MACROECONOMICS OF CLIMATE CHANGE IN A DUALISTIC ECONOMY

MACROECONOMICS OF CLIMATE CHANGE IN A DUALISTIC ECONOMY

A Regional General Equilibrium Analysis

SEVIL ACAR

EBRU VOYVODA

ERINÇ YELDAN

ACADEMIC PRESS

An imprint of Elsevier

Library of Congress Cataloging-in-Publication Data
A catalog record for this book is available from the Library of Congress

British Library Cataloguing-in-Publication Data
A catalogue record for this book is available from the British Library

ISBN: 978-0-12-813519-8

For information on all Academic Press publications visit our website at
https://www.elsevier.com/books-and-journals

  Working together
to grow libraries in
ELSEVIER Book Aid developing countries
International

www.elsevier.com • www.bookaid.org

Publisher: Candice Janco
Acquisition Editor: J. Scott Bentley
Editorial Project Manager: Brianna Garcia
Production Project Manager: Punithavathy Govindaradjane
Designer: Matthew Limbert

Typeset by Thomson Digital

CONTENTS

PREFACE

Scientists have reported that the surface temperature of our planet has increased by 0.9°C since the onset of the Industrial Revolution. They have also warned that life on Earth will face unforeseeable adverse consequences and be seriously threatened if the increase in surface temperature exceeds 2°C; thus, the scientific community set an ultimate target to limit the rise in global temperature by this amount (2°C). Scientists have estimated that a maximum of 450 ppm (parts per million molecules) of CO_2 should be released into the atmosphere to maintain this target. The atmosphere was estimated to hold 220 ppm of CO_2 at the time of the Industrial Revolution.

The total allowable CO_2 emission to contain the temperature rise at 2°C was calculated to be in the order of 2900 Gt (1 Gt = 1 billion tons). This was referred to as the global carbon budget, and approximately 1900 Gt of this allowance (65%) has already been spent. This leaves approximately 1000 Gt of allowable CO_2 emissions to limit global warming to 2°C. To meet this challenge, various nations came together in Paris, 2015, to share their intended nationally determined contributions with the international community. From that point onward, nations were free to exercise their "own" commitments to contribute to the global reduction of emissions to meet the 2°C (or more technically the 450 ppm) target.

Instruments of environmental policy have thus far mainly consisted of carbon tax-cum-subsidies and the administration of energy markets through taxation on both users and suppliers. However, it is well documented that the administration of price instruments through the market alone are not sufficient to achieve the broad objectives of controlling global greenhouse gas concentrations or maintaining a sustainable and ecofriendly growth path. Part of the problem is that the development of new ecofriendly technologies typically involves positive spillovers in the form of agglomeration effects, knowledge diffusion, cross-firm externalities, and industry-wide learning; however, the decentralized optimization embedded in the laissez-faire actions of the markets may fail to capture these positive spillovers. At the root of these problems are market failures, for which basic—economic and regulatory—instruments are available but not systematically used as part of broader policy packages.

Meanwhile, the most striking observations from the patterns of the global economy over the 21st century have been the deterioration of income distribution and the tendency for the middle classes to shrink. Income polarization and fragmentation have turned into the well-observed norms of global, and national, income stratification, as the share of global income by the upper one-thousandth super rich has hit social media.

In addition, with intensified pressures of unemployment looming everywhere, wage earners have witnessed a race to the bottom in terms of their remuneration, social rights, and working conditions. Complemented by the conservative policies invoking flexibility and privatization, global wage labor has suffered serious informalization and vulnerability, a deterioration in income distribution, and increased poverty. Global unemployment initially and primarily hit the young; for example, the International Labor Organization (ILO) reported that open unemployment among the youth (aged 15–24) reached 71 million in 2016 (ILO, 2016). However, the problems for the young are not limited to the threat of unemployment. The ILO warned that poverty also stands as a further serious threat, even to the young that are employed. It reported that 156 million young workers live under conditions of absolute poverty (defined as living on USD 3.10 per day), and disclosed that this figure covers 37.7% of young people in work (i.e., more than one-third).

Falling profitability in the industrial sectors and a global tendency toward deindustrialization were rampant over the 21st century. Investment expenditures on fixed capital stagnated and formed the basis of faltering productivity gains and rising structural unemployment. OECD statistics reported that labor productivity in many countries, particularly within the industrial sectors, was outright negative during the great recession, and this seems likely to persist into the third decade of the 21st century. Industrial labor productivity growth was reportedly nil in Latin America, while East Asia reportedly sustained (in a volatile manner) rates of labor productivity growth. These historical observations were carried over into the coming decades in an OECD (2014) Policy Paper, where it was projected that the global economy would likely slow down from its annual average of 3.6% during 2014–30 to 2.7% in 2030–60. It was also projected that the growth rate of today's developed world would slow to as little as 0.5% by 2060.

Increased poverty, reduced income distribution, and intensification of social exclusion and social violence have become the unavoidable outcomes as deindustrialization develops into a real threat for the future viability of the global economy. These outcomes were documented in the UNCTAD 2016 Trade and Development Report.

Thus it is clear that meeting the challenges of the 2°C economy requires the initiation of indigenous strategies of industrialization, energy use, and development that go beyond the tax–cum–subsidization interventions of the market apparatus. A new mode of development and energy utilization strategy is required to address: (1) issues of climate change and environmental abatement under the dualistic (fragmented) pathways of production and employment, and (2) the tendency for productivity patterns to fall. This study aims to pursue alternative visions of climate change and development economics that are comprehensive and broad enough to attain the multiple objectives of climate change mitigation, increased productivity, socially inclusive development pathways, and progressive income redistribution. It is our contention that global problems necessitate comprehensive strategies to address diverse—and yet interrelated—problems of climate change, poverty, duality, and faltering productivity.

Turkey is an emerging developing market economy with a dual structure (duality). The main features of this dual trap are explained by the coexistence of a "middle- or high-income Turkey," which is on its way to reach higher-income status, and a "poor Turkey," which aims to exit from the poverty trap and is in need of accelerated growth. This duality continuously breeds itself and enclaves "poor Turkey" within an eternal poverty trap. On one hand, this duality creates regional inequalities and fragmented/informalized industrial and labor market structures for the Turkish economy; however on the other, it also leads to environmental degradation and inefficiencies of the environmental policies designed to mitigate climate change. "High-income Turkey" relocates its production costs, which arise from the burden of high corporate taxes and environmental abatement regulations, toward "poor Turkey," and thus creates conditions of concerted urbanization alongside an unsustainable growth path where poverty and informalization are constantly reproduced.

The main focus of this study is the construction of a regional dynamic general equilibrium model, which accommodates the structure and dynamics of the dual trap embedded in the Turkish economy. It also aims to analyze the macroeconomic development policies designed at the regional level, and to investigate those policies aimed at the abatement of environmental pollution and climate change. The methodological section of the study performs this search with the aid of a two-region multisector macroeconomic general equilibrium model that has been constructed for the Turkish economy. The most important contributions of this construction, referred to as the Regional Computable General Equilibrium Modeling, are the decomposition of the national economy into its observed regional differences and its ability to generate a concrete impact analysis of the instruments of regional policy.

Therefore answers are sought to questions such as: (1) What will the regional employment and development impacts be of the "greening" policies of the Turkish economy in compliance with the key climate change targets within the Paris Agreement context?; (2) How will the patterns of production and employment be shaped in the strategic sectors of the Turkish economy (i.e., agriculture, automotive, construction, machine industry, and advanced services) over the course of greening and regional development?; and (3) What is the optimal mix of taxation, subsidization, and other policy instruments that will enable the Turkish economy to alleviate the duality trap, sustain its greening efforts, and mitigate climate change from the viewpoint of social welfare?

This effort has been a huge undertaking and required a collective team effort. We greatly acknowledge the help, motivation, and invaluable suggestions of our colleagues throughout this study. First and foremost, we thank our research assistants, Doğuhan Sundal, Gül Yücel, Yazgı Genç, Nihan Nur Akhan, Damla Durmaz, Reyhan Demir, and Kemal Göğebakan, for their devoted and diligent research assistance. We also thank Ümit Şahin, Ahmet Atıl Aşıcı, Mustafa Özgür Berke, Semra Cerit Mazlum, Levent Kurnaz, İzzet Arı, and our colleagues at Bilkent University, METU, and Altınbaş University for their comments and suggestions. Finally, we acknowledge the help given by the Elsevier editorial team, especially Brianna Garcia, Scott Bentley, Punitha Govindaradjane, and Swapna Praveen; working with them was an easy-going experience.

This research had been supported by a grant (114K941) from the Scientific and Technological Research Council of Turkey (TUBITAK), for which Sevil Acar and Erinç Yeldan acknowledge their gratitude.

REFERENCES

ILO, 2016. World Employment and Social Outlook. ILO, Geneva.
OECD, 2014. The Upcoming Slow Down of the Global Economy in the Next 60 Years. OECD, Paris.
UNCTAD, 2016. Trade and Development Report 2016. UNCTAD, Geneva.

CHAPTER 1

Introduction

Macroeconomics of Climate Change in a Dualistic Economy intends to construct a series of regional and dynamic general equilibrium models that accommodate the structure and dynamics of the dual trap embedded in the Turkish economy. These models include the analysis of macroeconomic development policies that are designed at the regional level, as well as those that are aimed at climate change abatement and mitigation. Recent studies have focused on environmental issues and have taken the macroeconomic structure of the modeled economies as given. We are of the opinion that by incorporating underlying characteristics of a dual economic structure, alongside questions of sustainability, increasing greenhouse gas (GHG) emissions, and income distribution, *Macroeconomics of Climate Change in a Dualistic Economy* can address questions, such as:

- What effects do energy and environmental policies in Turkey have on national and regional GHG emissions?
- What effects may "greening" policies of the Turkish economy have on regional employment and development patterns?
- How will patterns of production and employment be shaped in strategic sectors of the Turkish economy (i.e., agriculture, automotive, construction, machine industry, and advanced services) by "greening" and regional development?
- From the viewpoint of social welfare: What is the optimal mix of taxation, subsidization, and technology policies in the Turkish economy that will alleviate the duality trap, sustain "greening" efforts, and mitigate climate change?

The key contribution of *Macroeconomics of Climate Change in a Dualistic Economy* rests on addressing the issues of duality and environmental policy on climate change within a general equilibrium modeling approach. We therefore hope that the modeling will be of interest to students studying the macroeconomics of development, general equilibrium modeling, and the economics of climate change. The last topical area focuses on a burgeoning field surrounding policy debates on the 2°C target set by the UN and the participants of the widely-acclaimed COP meetings. Coupled with a discussion of recent advances in dynamic multiregional applied general equilibrium modeling, the proposed methodology is expected to be

Macroeconomics of Climate Change in a Dualistic Economy
http://dx.doi.org/10.1016/B978-0-12-813519-8.00001-7

of wide interest to graduate students, applied researchers, practitioners, and researchers from both the academic and public sectors.

1.1 BACKGROUND

Various aspects of sustained growth (or lack of) under regional fragmentation and patterns of duality have long been reported in the literature, especially regarding the structuralist tradition (Ros, 2000; Taylor, 1983, 2004). "Dual" economic structures have recently come to the forefront of the development economics literature, with seminal contributions from Fields (2004), Laitner (2000), and Temple (2005). In his survey of the concept for growth economists, Temple (2005) noted that "dual economy models (ought to) deserve a central place in the analysis of growth in developing countries (…) with factor misallocation, aggregate growth in the presence of factor market distortions, international differences in sectoral productivity, and the potential role of increasing returns to scale." Our investigation will go beyond the analyses of "traditional" dualism (based on differences in the wage rate from labor's marginal product in traditional agriculture) to encompass what Bertrand and Squire (1980) noted as "modern-sector dualism," with an advanced modern sector generating and sustaining traditional-sector conditions with a poverty trap based on informality and fragmentation.

Classic treatment of "Duality" was introduced to the literature with the dual-economy models of Fei and Ranis (1964) and Lewis (1954). Both visions highlighted the pathways of transitional growth via the transference of unlimited supplies of labor from traditional agriculture to modern industry. In their view, duality initially was referred as a diverse structure, which nevertheless followed a smooth adjustment toward modernity. As labor was lured from low-productivity (actually zero) traditional agriculture to high-productivity urban industries, growth occurred through lifting the masses toward a modern society.

However, over 50 years of research has clearly revealed that one of the striking feature of the mode of development is polarization of income per capita, which occurs across global, national, and regional economies. The expected smooth transition that destroys (creatively, according to Schumpeter? We doubt it!) traditionally stagnant rural economies, and moves masses out of poverty into the modern urban centers of growth, has not taken place. Globalization in the 20th century created miracles and disasters thus filling the ranks of what Colander termed as the bottom 1 billion, where daily per capita incomes fell below one dollar. Rates of growth were, on average, negative over the last quarter.

Such polarization was not limited across nations. Informalization, fragmentation, and social exclusion are indispensable outcomes of modern enclaves; in short, modern and formal centers of growth have simultaneously created and sustained fragmented informal bases. In Turkey, modern Istanbul not only retains and produces backwardness in Urfa, but also generates further Urfas within its geographical domain. As informal Urfas surround the Istanbul core, fragmented and dualistic activities form the basis of cheap labor sources and consist mainly of socially-excluded migrants who are, in turn, pressed to offer their labor power in "a race to the bottom." Turkey's experience is by no means unique. It is part of a larger picture of the international division of labor within the global economy, where formal and informal structures exist side by side as part of a larger social formation. In their study of the structural transformation of India's economy, Rada et al. (2012) noted that "a widening gap between India's skilled and well-paid on the one hand and those unskilled and mostly poor on the other hand has been on the rise." (p. 4). They further noted that "despite impressive expansion in production, job creation in the formal or organized sector has been meager for the last two decades. India's workforce remains employed in relatively low-productivity, low-pay jobs even if formal urban high-technology services output has expanded very rapidly." This has dire implications for social cohesion and the sustainability of growth (Breman, 2010; Chandrasekhar and Ghosh, 2007), where economic expansion is ultimately constrained by the hard boundaries of either lack of growth demand or the availability of skilled labor. With inequality at the regional and state levels becoming increasingly apparent, India seems to be trapped within the widening gaps between enclaves and backwardness (Deaton and Dréze, 2002). Similar observations have also been shared under diverse external conditions for Mexico, post-NAFTA. A McKinsey report (Bolio et al., 2014) described the Mexican structure as a "two-speed economy," with highly-productive industrial conglomerates with easy access to foreign technology and finance across the maquiladora belt of the US border coexisting with traditional family-owned small-scale businesses with almost stagnant labor productivity. These observations are in contrast to the well-defined, across-the-board conceptualizations of the classical duality theories, which suggested there would be sustained growth based on unlimited supplies of labor. However, further to these observations the enigma remains as, in the words of Reinert et al. (2016), "the profession's recent leaps into the mysteries of institutions' and 'human behavior' (failed to) solve the basic underlying problem of explaining why economic growth, by its nature, (has been) so uneven."

In our context, at least four clear-cut attributes of 21st century dualism come forward. The first pertains to the geographical location along the lines of classical periphery versus the core. The second pertains to access to technology, modern finance, and organizational management in firms and other production units. The underlying source of duality here does not necessarily rest on the different types of labor across skill levels, but, as a manifestation of the third attribute of modern duality, it is the direct outcome of heterogeneous capital formation. In the words of Mészáros (1995), "labor markets remain heterogeneous, because capital itself is heterogeneous." Heterogeneity of capital, along with the seemingly endless formation of subcontracting, off-shoring, etc., creates its own demand for heterogeneous labor types and causes deeply fragmented labor markets across organized formal sectors. We are therefore left with the fourth characteristic of dualism, which pertains to the persistence of fragmented regional peripheries due to the constraints of backward technologies, limited access to knowledge capital, and exclusion from modern or secular education. This encompasses all forms of social stratification along gender, ethnic, and religious castes. In this book we introduce various forms of sluggish interregional adjustment processes over both capital and relevant labor types. We incorporate various empirically-validated rigidities along the supply of informal labor, and modify the traditional assumption of a perfectly elastic long-run supply of rural labor in an unlimited population, as is seen in the conventional labor market duality.

Stifel and Thorbecke (2003) attempted to capture some of these elements through their characterization of a dual–dual economy, which included: (1) subsistence agriculture using traditional labor-intensive technologies; (2) commercial large-scale agricultural units using high-technology capital-intensive techniques; (3) an informal urban sector; and (4) urban modern industrial and service sectors.

We hinge on and extend this basic framework of duality by incorporating fragmentation across spatial forms of production and employment. Accommodation of migration is a further key feature of this social formation. Our approach here will be a multifaceted model of migration flow, allowing both skilled and unskilled labor from the poverty-trapped regions to join the ranks of vulnerability in the high-income regions. This specification goes well beyond traditional characterizations that lure rural labor surplus into the ranks of the higher-paid urban sectors and is designed to accommodate more complex migration traits, as this is both an economic and social phenomenon. In summary, our specification rests on the foundations of the regional location theory, empirical-based characterization of heterogeneous labor categories, and differentiated labor-supply responses along the fragmented factor markets. All of this can be cast in a dynamic framework driven by differentiated (lopsided) rates of productivity growth, stimulated through instruments of environmental abatement.

Fiscal policy and provision of public infrastructure constitute integral components of our abatement strategy. The role of public infrastructure investments in combatting regional growth bottlenecks is well documented (Conrad and Heng, 2002; Deepak et al., 2001; Giesecke, 2003). Our analysis will extend the arsenal of fiscal policy instruments to account for the objectives of abatement. Redirection of the (existing) subsidies to fossil fuels, invigoration of a carbon tax based on the polluter-pays principle, earmarking tax monies to targeted discretionary venues of pollution control, and expanding renewable energy sources are specific examples of the wide-ranging possibilities.

1.2 ON TURKEY

The methodological section of this study is performed with the aid of a multiregional multisector macroeconomic general equilibrium model. Referred to as regional computable general equilibrium modeling, the most important contributions of this construction are the decomposition of the national economy into its observed regional differences, and the generation of an impact analysis of the regional and environmental policy instruments. The choice of this focus was made for two reasons: First, as an emerging developing market economy, Turkey displays a dual structure (duality). The main features of the dual trap are revealed by the coexistence of a "middle–high income Turkey," which is on its way to reaching higher-income status, alongside a "poor Turkey," which is trying to exit from the poverty trap and is in need of accelerated growth. This spatial duality, which continuously breeds and enclaves "poor Turkey" within an eternal poverty trap, creates regional inequalities and a fragmented and informalized industry and labor market structure for the Turkish economy at large. It also leads to environmental degradation and renders the environmental policies for mitigating climate change inefficient. As "high income Turkey" relocates its production costs, which arise from the burden of high corporate taxes and environmental abatement regulations, toward "poor Turkey," it creates conditions of concerted urbanization and an unsustainable growth path in which poverty and informalization are continuously reproduced.

The second reason for this choice is that economic growth has generally not been decoupled from resource use and environmental quality. For example, a United Nations report (UN, 2013) noted that "the present dominant model of development is facing simultaneous multiple crises, such as depletion of natural resources and the market failures that have already marked the first decades of the current millennium." Therefore this model has been ineffective at enabling productive and decent employment and has exacerbated the phenomenon of climate change with its facets, including the depletion of natural resources, the loss of biodiversity, energy crisis, food security, etc. In contrast, the report underlines that the "green economy concept proposes to break away from the not very effective current model of development and move toward a more sustainable development paradigm that is merely characterized by low carbon emissions, rational use of resources and social inclusiveness." These observations are central to green growth, a relatively new concept that has captured the attention of global policy makers, researchers, and civil society organizations, which could help to design and evaluate policies that could efficiently achieve environmental sustainability. This is of particular interest to fast-growing emerging market economies, which are characterized by rapidly increasing ecological footprints, and which seek to decouple economic growth from rising energy use and pollution.

The lack of decoupling is also observable in Turkey. As of 2015, Turkey's per capita emissions of carbon dioxide (CO_2) and other GHGs (CO_2 eq.) stood at around 6 tons, while its total CO_2 eq. emissions per GDP (in constant USD) reached 0.524 kg. Turkey displays relatively low emission figures in comparison to global and OECD averages; however, it is cited in the top five countries with the fastest growing rates of aggregate CO_2 eq. emissions. Turkey's CO_2 eq. emissions increased from 214 to 475 million tons in the period from 1990 to 2015 (a cumulative increase of 122%), and are expected to increase to 675 million tons by 2030. This suggests that Turkey will be on a divergent trend to many of the emerging market developing economies as well as to the world average over the coming decades (Acar and Yeldan, 2016).

Environmental policy instruments in Turkey have thus far consisted of carbon tax-cum-subsidies and administering high taxes through the energy markets, both to the user and the supplier. However, it is well-documented that the administration of price instruments through the market alone is not sufficient to control global GHG concentrations or maintain a sustainable and eco-friendly growth path (Acar et al., 2014). Part of the problem is that the development of novel eco-friendly technologies typically involves positive spillovers in the form of agglomeration effects, knowledge diffusion, cross-firm externalities, and industry-wide learning; however, the decentralized optimization embedded in the laissez-faire actions of the markets may fail to capture these positive spillovers. Market failures are at the root of these problems, as although basic (economic and regulatory) instruments are available, their systematic use in broader policy packages have been lacking.

Considering the lack of an adequate modeling paradigm for environmental policy analysis in Turkey, the effectiveness of policy interventions and their economic impacts are not well-known. Hence there is a strong need for the construction and utilization of analytical models that can account for the general equilibrium effects of environmental policy analysis.

1.3 OBJECTIVES

The literature regarding classical development has emphasized the relationship between economic growth and changes in the production structure. It also allocates special properties to industry and the process of industrialization in its capacity to create and combine a series of complementarities, scale properties, and external economies to generate a sustainable cycle of resource mobilization, increased productivity, rising demand, increased income, and economic growth.

Developments in the global economy have contributed to renewed discussions on the role of structural transformation in achieving sustained economic growth and development. Other factors that have added to this discussion include the catch-up failure of many developing regions, which are often associated with "traps" and downturns (i.e., low-development traps, middle-income traps, and premature deindustrialization); the end of the windfall export gains led by the commodity price boom in the 2000s; and the continued vulnerability of many developing regions to external shocks (UNCTAD, 2016).

The dual relationship between climate change and development serves as yet another important factor. For example, climate change creates serious challenges for development; however, the priorities of economic growth and development also have major consequences on climate change and vulnerability. In its basic form, emission control and effective mitigation require massive transformations in production and energy systems, such as moving away from traditional high-carbon energy sources (i.e., a phase-out of coal or gas-fueled power plants and fossil fuel subsidies), increasing fuel efficiency, broadly deploying advanced renewable technologies, and implementing measures to increase energy efficiency (IEA, 2008).

Given the overall scope, we propose the concrete objectives of this study are:

- to use the analytical findings in the literature regarding technological change and innovation in response to environmental pollution abatement and climate change mitigation (Goulder and Schneider, 1999; Löschel, 2002; Porter and van der Linde, 1995), technology path (Aghion, 2014; Aghion et al., 2011, 2012), and duality (OECD, 2014; Temple, 2005) to construct a dynamic small "open economy" general equilibrium model for the regional Turkish economies, which can be utilized for the analysis of policies of regional development and environmental abatement;
- to evaluate the environmental tax or subsidy policies, the policies for promoting sustainable and equitable regional growth, and the policies for employment and investment under the resource constraints and the social welfare criteria; and
- to decompose the dynamic growth path of the Turkish economy and the climate-related problems that are likely to be faced along this path using a long-term time horizon encompassing the 2010s.

Previous research regarding these questions has typically been conducted within a macroeconomic environment where the analyzed economy is regarded as a homogenous entity. Conversely, evidence on global capitalism for the 21st century suggests that growth over the next century will be erratic and highly uneven. For example, a recent OECD (2014) report claims that the world economy will significantly decline over the next 60 years. OECD researchers argue that two important factors of this prognostication will be: (1) the duality and unevenness of income distribution across functional and regional sites, with a consequent rise of social exclusion and conflict; and (2) environmental degradation due to the threat of climate change. This manuscript aims to address these two issues simultaneously within the discipline of general equilibrium, and attempts to provide an analytical quest into viable alternatives using real world data for an indigenous economy, Turkey, in a dynamic framework. We believe that this will serve as the unique identifier of this manuscript.

1.4 OUTLINE OF THIS MANUSCRIPT

The remaining sections of the book are as follows:

Chapter 2 is devoted to understanding the dual characteristics of economies and growth patterns within the context of development challenges in the 21st century. This will be performed for both developing countries in general and more specifically for Turkey. The broad contours of growth and adjustments in the global economy before, during, and after the 2008–09 global crises are initially identified. Second, structural sources of deindustrialization, widening duality in labor markets, and technological diffusion are addressed. Third, all of the aforementioned observations are linked with the macroeconomics of global climate change and the implications for resource use and environmental degradation. A key hypothesis of this chapter is that the projected lack of decoupling between growth and GHG emissions is mostly driven by the dualistic patterns of growth and industrialization across Turkey. Yeldan et al. (2014) suggest that the main causes of the productivity slowdown in the Turkish economy over the 2010s are the diverging patterns of regional development and the widening gap between high- and low-income regions, as well as modern versus traditional sectoral production (and consumption) patterns. In this chapter the fragmented nature of the commodity and labor markets across regional Turkey is documented. We argue that the fragmented dualistic structure is maintained within the current macroeconomic path of Turkey, as is the continued informalization of both the capital and labor markets and the diverging growth across regions.

Based on the economic structure laid out in Chapter 2, Chapter 3 argues that the lack of mitigation at the national level is manifested by the widening gap across regional GHG emissions, which is caused by the dual economic structure and the differential subsidization schemes across the regions. This chapter dissects and interprets the existing statistics related to energy and climate change in Turkey. It also provides an account of the legal background, strategy documents, and policies related to energy and the environment (i.e., fossil fuel subsidies and feed-in tariffs for renewable energy). In addition, it casts light on the possible extensions of environmental policies from the voluntary carbon markets and the Partnership for Market Readiness project in Turkey. Finally, this chapter has been extended to include the post-Paris agreement era for climate change and to undertake an international comparison of developing countries with respect to climate change policies.

Chapter 4 introduces the main components of the applied general equilibrium model designed for Turkey. It discusses its distinguishing features and its contribution to the modeling literature with a unique emphasis on duality, regionalization, and social relevance. It further conceptualizes a social accounting matrix for the regionally fragmented dual economy to accommodate Turkish macrolevel data. Given the theoretical structure of the computable general equilibrium (CGE) model, the main data sources of the modeling paradigm are introduced and tabulated within the discipline of Walrasian general equilibrium. The unique contribution of this chapter is its accommodation of regional differentiation and dualistic labor markets and its preparation for the database in social accounting matrix format. This chapter purports to extend traditional neoclassical (Walrasian) growth modeling (based on one-sector depictions of the aggregate economy) with a balanced growth path notion toward the steady state. As such, we aim to contribute to the empirics of the traditional growth paradigm by questioning the long-run equilibrium pathway toward a balanced steady state.

Finally, Chapter 5 introduces various policy scenarios and tests them for equitable and sustained regional development, mitigation of climate change, and provision of green growth.

The existing environmental policies in Turkey are mainly comprised of gasoline and fuel taxes. Conversely, Turkey continues to support coal mining and coal-fired power generation with the aim of utilizing all its domestic coal resources in the near future. Since coal subsidies work against the competitiveness of renewable energy technologies, the energy sector has been locked in to the continuation of fossil fuel-based systems, and thus the investment decisions of renewable energy investors have been heavily jeopardized (Bridle and Kitson, 2014). Eliminating coal subsidies and redirecting these funds toward renewable energy, green jobs, or CO_2 mitigation will likely improve efficiency and social welfare.

One of our key hypotheses is that coal subsidies could be phased out and fiscal savings from this, as well as the additional revenue from carbon taxation schemes, could be used to develop renewable energy and energy efficiency while simultaneously mitigating the environmentally harmful impacts. Coal subsidy phaseout and carbon taxation would decrease CO_2 emissions, increase fiscal revenues, and potentially generate green energy and green jobs. Switching from subsidization of coal and other fossil fuels to supporting the development of renewables is expected to be a win–win–win strategy for a cleaner environment, a decreased dependence on fuel imports, and an expansion of renewables in electricity production. In addition, alternative public policy intervention mechanisms could be developed to accelerate technology adoption and energy efficiency and achieve higher employment, energy security, and sustainable growth patterns.

In the search for viable alternative policy instruments to complement efforts of greening and decarbonizing the economy, the last chapter intends to use a dynamic and regionally-differentiated applied general equilibrium model. This model will investigate the impacts of various policy instruments, such as the removal of fossil fuel subsidies, the introduction of a carbon tax, the development of a "renewables sector" via induced technology, and the investment in research and development devoted to the stimulation of such efforts toward a greener economy.

REFERENCES

Acar, S., Challe, S., Christopoulos, S., Christo, G., 2014. Fossil fuel subsidies as a lose-lose: fiscal and environmental burdens in Turkey. Paper presented at the 14th IAEE European Energy Conference, October 28–31, 2014, Rome, Italy.

Acar, S., Yeldan, E., 2016. Environmental impacts of coal subsidies in Turkey: a general equilibrium analysis. Energy Policy 90, 1–15.

Aghion, P., 2014. Industrial policy for green growth. Paper presented at the 17th World Congress of the International Economics Association, Jordan.

Aghion, P., Boulanger, J., Cohen, E., 2011. Rethinking Industrial Policy, Bruegel Policy Brief.

Aghion, P., Dechezleprêtre, A., Hemous, D., Martin, R., van Reenen, J., 2012. Carbon taxes, path dependency and directed technical change: evidence from the auto industry. NBER Working Paper No. 18596.

Bertrand, T., Squire, L., 1980. The relevance of the dual economy model: a case study of Thailand. Oxf. Econ. Pap. 32 (3), 480–511.

Bolio, E., Remes, J., Lajous, T., Manyika, J., Rossé, M., Ramirez, E., 2014. A tale of two Mexicos: growth and prosperity in a two-speed economy. McKinsey Global Institute. Available from: https://www.canback.com/files/2014_MK_MGI_Mexico_Full_report.pdf.

Breman, J., 2010. India's social question in a state of denial. Econ. Polit. Wkly. 45, 42–46.

Bridle, R., Kitson, L., 2014. The impact of fossil-fuel subsidies on renewable electricity generation. Global Subsidies Initiatives Report, December 2014. Available from: http://www.iisd.org/sites/default/...les/publications/impact-fossil-fuel-subsidiesrenewable-electricity-generation.pdf.

Chandrasekhar, C.P., Jayati Ghosh., 2007. Recent employment trends in India and China: an unfortunate convergence? Soc. Scientist 35, 19–46.

Conrad, K., Heng, S., 2002. Financing road infrastructure by savings in congestion costs: a CGE analysis. Ann. Reg. Sci. 36, 107–122.

Deaton, A., Dréze, J., 2002. Poverty and inequality in India: a reexamination. Econ. Polit. Wkly. 7, 3729–3748.

Deepak, M.S., Taylor West, C., Spreen, T.H., 2001. Local government portfolios and regional growth: some combined dynamic CGE/optimal control results. J. Reg. Sci. 41, 291–354.

Fei, J.C.H., Ranis, G., 1964. Development of the Labor Surplus Economy. Homewood, Irwin, United States.

Dualism in the labor market: a perspective on the Lewis model after half a century. Available from: http://digitalcommons.ilr.cornell.edu/articles/268/.

Giesecke, J., 2003. Targeting regional output with state government fiscal instruments: a dynamic multi-regional CGE analysis. Aust. Econ. Pap. 42, 214–233.

Goulder, L.H., Schneider, S., 1999. Induced technological change, crowding out and the attractiveness of CO2 emissions abatement. Resour. Environ. Econ. 21 (3–4), 211–253.

IEA, 2008. World Energy Outlook. International Energy Agency, Paris.

Laitner, J., 2000. Structural change and economic growth. Rev. Econ. Stud. 67 (3), 545–571.

Lewis, W.A., 1954. Economic development with unlimited supplies of labour. Manchester Sch. 22 (2), 139–191.

Löschel, A., 2002. Technological change in economic models of environmental policy: a survey. Ecol. Econ. 43, 105–126.

Mészáros, 1995. Beyond Capital. Monthly Review Press, New York, United States.

OECD, 2014. Policy challenges for the next 50 years. OECD Economic Policy Paper, July, No. 9. Available from: http://www.oecd.org/economy/growth/Policy-challenges-for-the-next-fiftyyears.pdf.

Porter, M.E., van der Linde, C., 1995. Toward a new conception of the environment-competitiveness relationship. J. Econ. Perspect. 9 (4), 97–118.

Rada, C., von Arnim, R., 2014. India's structural transformation and role in the world economy. J. Policy Model. 36, 1–23.

Reinert, E., Endresen, S., Ianos, I., Saltelli, A., 2016. Epilogue: the future of economic development between utopias and dystopias. In: Reinert, E., Ghosh, J., Kattel, R. (Eds.), Handbook of Alternative Theories of Economic Development. Edward Elgar Press, Northampton, United States.

Ros, J., 2000. Development Theory and the Economics of Growth. University of Michigan, Ann Arbor, United States.

Stifel, D., Thorbecke, E., 2003. A dual-dual CGE model of an archetype African economy: trade, reform, migration and poverty. J. Policy Model. 25, 207–235.

Taylor, L., 1983. Structuralist Macroeconomics. University Press, London, Cambridge, United Kingdom.

Taylor, L., 2004. Reconstructing Macroeconomics: Structuralist Proposals and Critiques of the Mainstream. Harvard University Press, Massachusetts, London.

Temple, J., 2005. Dual economy models: a primer of growth economists. Manchester Sch. 73 (4), 435–478.

UN, 2013. The 16th Session of the Intergovernmental Committee Experts of West Africa (inclusive green growth to accelerate socio-economic development in West Africa), Coté d'ivorie.

UNCTAD, 2016. Trade and Development Report, Geneva.

Yeldan, A.E., Taşçı, K., Voyvoda, E., Özsan, E., 2014. Planning for regional development: a general equilibrium analysis for Turkey. In: Yülek, M. (Ed.), Economic Planning and Industrial Policy in the Globalizing Economy. Springer, Heidelberg, New York, Dordrecht, London.

FURTHER READING

Acar, S., Kitson, L., Bridle, R., 2015. Subsidies to coal and renewable energy in Turkey. Global Subsidies Initiative Report, March 2015.

CHAPTER 2

Patterns of Growth in Dual Economies: Challenges of Development in the 21st Century

Literature regarding the basics of classical development emphasizes on the relationship between economic growth and changes in production structure. It also allocates special properties to industry, and more specifically to the ability of industrialization to create and combine a series of complementarities, scale properties, and external economies to generate a sustainable cycle of resource mobilization, increasing productivity, rising demand, income, and economic growth.

Changes in the global economy have contributed to the renewed discussions on the role of structural transformation in achieving sustained economic growth and development. The catch-up failure of many developing regions, which are often associated with "traps" and downturns (i.e., low-development traps, middle-income traps, and premature deindustrialization); the end of windfall export gains led by the commodity price boom in 2000s; and the continued vulnerability of many developing regions to external shocks have also added to this discussion (UNCTAD, 2016).

The dual relationship between climate change and development serves as yet another important factor. On one hand, the effects of climate change create serious challenges to development; however, on the other hand, prioritization of economic growth and development has had major consequences on climate change and vulnerability. In its basic form, emission control and effective mitigation require not only the transformation of production systems but also the transformation of energy systems, including moving away from traditional high-carbon energy sources (a phase-out of coal-fueled power plants), increasing fuel efficiency, deploying advanced renewable technologies, and implementing measures to increase energy efficiency (IEA, 2008).

This chapter attempts to bring all of these elements together within the context of developmental challenges for the 21st century. To this end, the broad contours of growth and adjustments in the global economy are

Macroeconomics of Climate Change in a Dualistic Economy
http://dx.doi.org/10.1016/B978-0-12-813519-8.00002-9

studied before, during, and after the 2008–09 global crisis. Four general patterns emerge from this analysis including the stagnation of wage incomes, the declining investment efforts, the consequent decline in the growth rates of productivity, and the compensatory rise in corporate and household indebtedness. This chapter continues with a deeper investigation of the structural sources of deindustrialization and the widening duality in both labor markets and technological diffusion. Finally, these ideas are linked with the macroeconomics of global climate change and the implications of the feedback effects of the economy, resource-use, and environmental-degradation nexus.

2.1 PATTERNS OF GROWTH AND ADJUSTMENT IN THE GLOBAL ECONOMY

The 21st century began with prolonged recession, lopsided growth, and widening income inequalities, consequently producing social exclusion, segmentation, and escalating regional social conflicts. The eruption of the financial crisis in the United States in September 2008 produced negative growth rates and led to the total collapse of global product in 2009, the first time this had happened since the great depression in the 1930s. The ensuing adjustment pathways did not bring the expected recovery, as the centers of the global economy and its peripheries drifted into stagnation and mounting debt and experienced rising inequalities in income and wealth, deepening segmentation of precarious global working environments, and increased dualities along formal and informal jobs.

These factors led to this period being termed the great recession, and highlighted the prolonged strains of missing spikes of new growth and the turtle habitat of the global economic system. Since the start of the crisis, the average annual rate of growth of per capita income of the world economy has averaged 1.5%. This is a noticeable slowdown against the so-called "golden era" of global capitalism, which roughly encompassed the post-World War II period. Of note is the decline in the rate of per capita income growth in the developed world, which fell from an average of 3.5% during 1950–80 to 1.1% during the post-2009 great recession.

Although the average growth rate of per capita income seems to have increased for the developing world as a whole (Table 2.1), this is observed to be mostly contained to China and other Asian economies. In contrast, a decline in the growth rate by more than 50% was observed

Table 2.1 Per capita income growth rates (%) in the world economy

	1951–80	1981–2015	2001–10	2010–15
Developed economies	3.5	1.8	1.2	1.1
United States	2.3	1.8	0.9	1.4
Developing economies	2.7	3.8	5.8	4.0
Africa	1.8	1.2	3.0	1.8
Latin America	2.6	1.3	2.4	1.1
Asia	2.8	5.0	7.0	4.9
China	2.3	7.7	11.1	7.2
Global	2.7	2.1	2.1	1.5

Source: UNCTAD, 2016. Trade and Development Report. Structural Transformation for Inclusive and Sustained Growth. United Nations publications, New York and Geneva; TDR, Table 2.2.

for Latin America, and divergence for the sub-Saharan African economies (Tables 2.2 and 2.3).

This "new normal" has set the stage as a new vocabulary has emerged to characterize the dilemmas of attempting to narrate isolated (and unsustained) episodes of growth within an overall mass of stagnation and income polarization. For example, traditional concepts of "developing economies" or "industrial and finance capital" became neutral terms, such as "emerging markets" or "market players." New mystified jargon such as "Quantitative easing," "decoupling," and "the zero bound" have also been implemented

A thorough explanation of the nature and causes of the great recession is beyond the focus of this study. Nevertheless, it is pertinent to identify its distinguishing (and structural) features including the stagnation of wages, the declining investment effort, the decline in the rates of productivity growth, and the rise in corporate and household indebtedness.

2.1.1 Stagnant or Falling Real Wages Across the Global Economy

The collapse of the Soviet system and the opening of the Chinese and Indian markets on the global platform have together added 1.5 billion new workers to the global economically-active labor force. This has led to a doubling of the labor force and a reduction of the global capital-labor ratio by 50%. With the intensified pressures of unemployment, wage earners have witnessed a "race to the bottom," in terms of their wage remunerations, social rights, and working conditions. Complemented by neoliberal policies invoking flexibility and privatization, the global labor force had suffered serious informalization and vulnerability, deterioration of income distribution, and increased poverty.

Table 2.2 Nonfinancial corporations: investment expenditures and debt indicators (%)

	Investment expenditures/profits			Investment expenditures/ capital stock			Debt/total sales volume			Debt/fixed assets		
	1995–2002	2003–08	2009–14	1995–2002	2003–08	2009–14	1995–2002	2003–09	2010–14	1995–2002	2003–09	2010–14
Argentina	121.2	91.9	104.9	11.9	9.2	17.5	71.8	46.2	27.7	48.5	43.8	41.0
Brazil	178.2	104.3	79.8	14.1	19.1	18.0	53.5	47.4	59.1	45.3	67.0	76.5
Chile	107.2	109.5	92.7	11.3	9.6	9.1	95.0	54.2	57.4	52.1	53.6	71.8
China	131.2	164.9	105.7	14.2	16.3	16.4	64.6	37.2	39.8	59.0	53.7	75.4
India	122.0	127.5	114.3	20.7	25.7	19.4	46.4	34.9	48.6	71.4	67.0	87.2
Indonesia	109.8	89.4	81.0	16.2	10.7	15.6	111.2	50.5	40.8	105.6	76.7	73.7
Malaysia	88.8	72.3	55.3	11.2	7.8	8.2	81.6	59.2	54.8	77.3	69.2	69.5
Mexico	98.2	92.4	89.2	10.3	10.5	11.4	47.0	39.9	46.5	45.8	56.9	78.4
Korea	287.8	103.6	106.8	14.3	11.2	10.6	50.5	30.8	30.8	104.2	71.5	78.5
Russia	217.7	134.0	83.2	26.8	10.4	10.6	111.0	77.7	58.6	4.0	30.0	17.2
South Africa	83.3	73.4	65.8	23.5	29.9	19.6	14.8	20.7	25.4	42.0	46.0	48.1
Thailand	84.6	71.5	58.9	10.5	13.0	13.3	103.9	38.2	32.5	119.1	75.5	78.1
Turkey	138.9	73.1	69.1	54.1	13.3	14.0	22.9	27.7	36.6	80.9	83.4	106.6

Table 2.3 Investment expenditures and average labor products in selected countries

	Rate of growth investment expenditures (%)					Rate of growth of average labor productivity (%)					Rate of Growth of Labor Product in Industry (%)				
	1970–79	1980–89	1990–99	2000–07	2010–14	1970–79	1980–89	1990–99	2000–07	2010–14	1970–79	1980–89	1990–99	2000–07	2010–14
Developed economies	3.4	2.5	2.6	4.8	0.9	3.1	1.8	1.6	2.1	0.8	2.5	2.8	3.1	2.8	1.1
Sub-Saharan Africa	4.2	−0.8	1.9	9.1	7.4	1.8	0.3	0.6	2.9	2.3	0	−0.2	−0.7	0.5	2.7
Latin America	7.1	−2.8	5.2	5.9	5.4	1.9	−2.0	1.2	1.3	1.5	1.3	−1.7	2.2	1.5	0.0
Argentina	3	−7	9.7	6.6	2.0	1.2	−2.8	3.7	0.3	2.2	1.7	−1.4	6.9	−0.7	−2.5
Brazil	9.4	−1.6	1.8	2.6	1.8	4.2	−1.2	1.3	0.8	0.8	3.4	−2.8	2.9	0.0	−2.5
Chile	−1.0	4.4	7.3	8.3	5.2	1.3	−0.8	3.8	1.7	1.7	−0.3	−0.5	6.2	0.1	−1.8
Mexico	7.3	−2.7	4.8	3	3.2	1.3	−1.6	0.1	0.8	1.3	0.6	−1.7	0.4	0.6	3.7
East Asia	10.4	8.7	6.8	14.1	9.3	3.0	6.3	6.3	6.0	4.2	0.8	4.9	9.1	6.4	5.1
China	7.2	6.5	13.8	12.5	8.1	1.2	6.5	7.8	8.7	7.2	−1.6	4.8	10.4	7.1	6.9
Korea	16.3	11.0	4.5	3.7	1.7	4.7	6.1	4.9	3.3	1.2	3.2	5.0	7.7	5.6	4.3
South East Asia	10.8	5.0	2.4	4.7	5.7	3.6	2.4	2.6	2.8	3.2	2.5	1.5	1.8	2.5	1.8
Indonesia	13.6	7.4	1.3	6.7	6.6	3.7	1.9	1.8	3.2	4.9	3.2	−0.4	2.3	2.4	0.8
Malaysia	14.2	4.7	4.0	3.7	9.1	4.8	2.5	3.5	3.0	1.9	0.2	2.0	0.9	4.0	1.6
The Philippines	10.4	−0.5	1.7	3.1	7.0	1.9	−1.0	0.1	2.1	4.8	4	−2.9	−1.0	1.9	3.7
Thailand	6.5	8.6	−3.5	7.4	2.7	5.3	4.6	4.4	3.2	2.8	2.5	5.9	2.3	1.9	1.1
South Asia	6.5	3.1	5.6	8.1	4.7	1.3	1.8	2.6	2.8	3.8	1.8	1.2	3.1	1.3	3.0
India	3.9	6.3	6.8	12.5	3.8	0.5	1.8	2.9	4.1	5.0	2.3	1.3	0.7	3.3	0.5
West Asia	10.7	−0.8	3.1	10.8	−2	2.9	−3.5	0.4	1.2	−1.7	3.0	−2.1	1.4	2.6	−1.5
Turkey	4.4	9.2	3.0	6.8	2.2	2.6	2.5	1.1	4.0	1.2	5.0	−0.4	0.6	2.6	−0.3

Source: UNCTAD, 2016. Trade and Development Report. Structural Transformation for Inclusive and Sustained Growth. United Nations publications, New York and Geneva; TDR.

Global unemployment initially hit the young. For example, in its 2016 World Employment and Social Outlook, the International Labor Organization (ILO) reported that open unemployment in those aged 15–24 had reached 71 million. Of these, 53.5 million resided in the newly emerging market economies, the so-called dynamic manufacturers of the world. The rate of youth unemployment in these economies was estimated to be 13.6%, while the global average stood at 13.1%

Problems for the young are not limited to the threat of unemployment. According to the ILO report, poverty was also a serious threat to those youths who were unable to find a job. The ILO reported that 156 million young workers lived under conditions of absolute poverty. Researchers set the limit of absolute poverty at USD 3.10 per day, and found that this figure amounted to 37.7% of those who were employed. Therefore one-third of the employed youth were working under conditions of absolute poverty.

The declining trend in wage remunerations is most vividly seen for the US economy in Fig. 2.1. In this figure the hourly real wage rates in US private manufacturing are contrasted against real labor productivity throughout the post–World War II period. During 1950–80 the rise of real wages was in tandem with productivity; however, 1980 changed

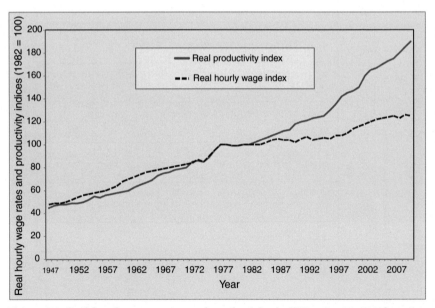

Figure 2.1 *Real hourly wage rates and productivity in USA private manufacturing (1982=100). (Modified from Economic Policy Institute, Washington DC. http://www.epi. org/productivity-pay-gap/).*

this scenario and signaled a different regime in the global economy. This is depicted best in David Harvey's seminal observation that "something significant has changed in the way capitalism has been working since about 1970" (Harvey, 1989, p. 192).

As Fig. 2.1 attests, the link between labor productivity and real wages was broken after 1980. This was known as the "age of neoliberal reform," which was characterized by increased flexibility of the labor markets, a reduced role of the social welfare state, and an intensified commercialization of the public services. However, what lay at the heart of this restructuring was the ascendancy of finance over industry, a global process of financialization, which imposed its logic of short-termism, liquidity, flexibility, and mobility over the objectives of long-term industrialization, sustainable development, and poverty alleviation within social welfare-driven states. Financialization is a loose term, and no consensus exists among economists on its definition. In line with Arrighi's The Long Twentieth Century, Krippner (2005, p. 172) defined it as a pattern of accumulation in which profits accrue primarily through financial channels rather than through trade and commodity production. Epstein (2005, p. 3) stated that "financialization means the increasing role of financial motives, financial markets, financial actors and financial institutions in the operation of domestic and international economies." In the following chapter, financialization is considered as a phenomenon, which is described by increasing financial motives, and the volume and impact of financial activities within and among countries.

A large number of developing countries have suffered deindustrialization, informalization, and worsening of the position of wage labor under these conditions, thus resulting in a deterioration of income distribution and increased poverty. Many of these phenomena have occurred in tandem with the onset of neoliberal reform, which has imposed the rapid liberalization of trade and the premature deregulation of indigenous financial markets. Thus all economies (industrialized or peripheral) have experience wage income collapses and a fall in the income share of wage labor in aggregate domestic products. This could only have been sustained via increased indebtedness and speculative ventures and not investments in real fixed capital.

The concomitant erosion of incomes has been a common observation in all the global economies. A direct reflection of this assessment is portrayed in Fig. 2.2, where the wage income share (as a ratio of respective GDP levels) is documented. The figure uses data from the UN AMECO database and shows that income compensation for almost all

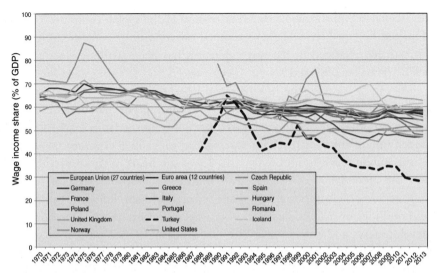

Figure 2.2 *Adjusted wage share: total economy: as percentage of GDP at current market prices (compensation per employee as percentage of GDP at market prices per person employed). (Data taken from European Commission Economic and Financial Affairs, AMECO database).*

major economies has been on a declining trend since the early 1970s. The decline of wage costs is expected to lead to a general tendency of the rise of profitability of capital.

2.1.2 The Consequent Rise in Profitability did not Lead to the Warranted Investment Push

Evidence supports the proposition that the post-1980 period offered a viable environment for expanding the profitability of global capital. For example, Orhangazi (2008) supported his theories of financialization of the US economy using his calculation of the profit rate in nonfinancial corporations over the postwar era. Orhangazi reported a secular decline of the profit rates of the nonfinancial corporations after the second half of the 1980s. After an extended period of restructuring during the 1980s, under the supply-side economics of Ronald Reagan and Paul Volcker, the profitability was observed to rise. Orhangazi's findings were also supported by the work of Duménil and Lévy (2001, 2004). In their analysis of the profitability of capital in the United States and Europe, they reported the behavior of the rate of profit (as measured by the ratio of net product minus total cost of labor) to the value of the stock of physical capital. Their data corroborated Orhangazi's findings with even more pronounced tendencies. As clearly

Figure 2.3 *Profit rate in the private sector, USA and Europe. (Duménil, G., Lévy, D., 2001. Costs and benefits of neoliberalism. A class analysis. Rev. Int. Political Econ. 8 (4), 578–607).*

shown in Fig. 2.3, the post-1980 patterns of profitability revealed a breakthrough for private capital returns in United States and Europe.

What is hidden beneath the path of aggregate profitability in Fig. 2.3 is the financialization of the patterns of accumulation. To fully account for the divergent patterns of finance over industrial profitability, Fig. 2.4A and B shows yet another aspect: it was actually the rise of financial returns that increased aggregate profitability. As stagnation of industrial profit rates deepened, the rise of financial profit opportunities compensated for such losses. Financialization was then the major response of capital in its quest for expansion, profits, and further expansion.

It was at this juncture that the introduction of debt instruments under post-1980 financialization enabled the middle classes to become a component of final demand. During a period of falling incomes, newly created debt instruments helped the American (and other economies) working class to become part of the consumerist culture. As the level of private savings to the gross domestic product fell to negative ratios, household debts rapidly accumulated. Therefore financialization was opportune, not only in terms of compensating the loss of industrial profitability, but also for expanding the consumption power for middle-income households that would have otherwise experienced significant income losses.

Data from the Bank of Settlements revealed that nongovernmental corporate debt accumulation has been the driving force behind this episode.

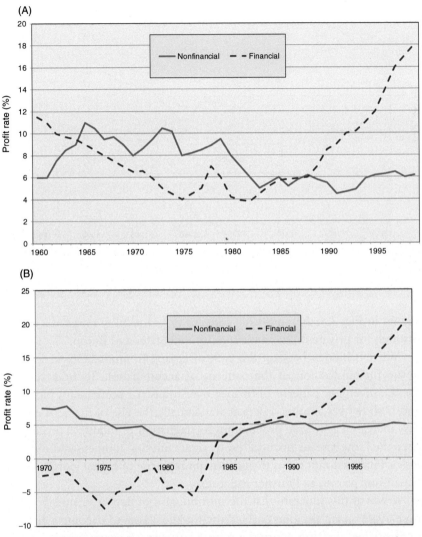

Figure 2.4 *(A) US: Profit rate of nonfinancial corporations. (B) France: profit rate of nonfinancial and financial corporations. (Duménil, G., Lévy, D., 2001. Costs and benefits of neoliberalism. A class analysis. Rev. Int. Political Econ. 8 (4), 578–607).*

Accordingly, nonfinancial corporate debt in the developing emerging market economies rose from USD 9 trillion in 2008 to USD 25 trillion in 2015, almost doubling as a ratio to GDP from 57% to 104% (Table 2.2). Taking data from selected economies in Table 2.2, the basic message is that investment expenditures have been on a declining trend in comparison to both aggregate returns to capital (profits) and the installed levels of capital stock.

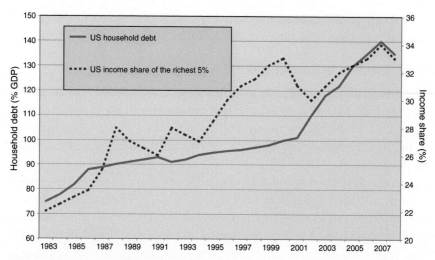

Figure 2.5 USA household debt and income share of the richest 5%. *(Modified from Michael Robert: Is inequality the cause of capitalist crises? Available from: http:// thenextrecession.wordpress.com/).*

The most rapid declines were observed in countries, such as Korea, Turkey, and Russia; however, no country has displayed an opposing (positive) trend. The third and fourth column blocks in Table 2.2 reveal that accumulated debt has fallen against total sales, but has risen against fixed assets.

Another characteristic of the debt problem has been the positive correlation between the rise of household debt and income concentration at the upper scale. Data on US household debt reveals that (as a ratio to GDP) it rose from 75% in the early 1980s to in excess of 130% by the end of 2010. As a parallel development, a rise in the income share of the richest 5% of the population was observed from 22% to 34% (Fig. 2.5).

These observations lead us to propose that, on the one hand, indebtedness enabled the maintenance of effective demand despite falling incomes and declining productivity; however, it also led to the expansion of casino capitalism as new financial instruments were created and the global financial markets turned into a melting soup.

Meanwhile, the advent of financialization led to the short-term and highly-volatile expansion of hot finance. With the ascendance of finance over industry, loanable funds were provided for the expansion of lucrative products of speculative finance. Investment expenditures on fixed capital also stagnated and formed the basis for the faltering productivity gains and expanding structural unemployment. Increasing poverty levels, worsening income distribution, and intensification of social exclusion and social violence were the unavoidable outcomes as deindustrialization became a real threat to the viable future of the global economy.

2.1.3 Decline in Productivity

The divergence of investment priorities away from industry toward speculative finance has taken its toll on fixed investments in the global economy, especially in industry. The overall decline in fixed investments was observed to be one of the "stylized facts" of the first 2 decades of the 21st century. As documented in Table 2.3, the growth rate of fixed investment expenditure in the developed world slowed significantly from an annualized rate of 3.4% in the 1970s to less than 1.0% during 2010–14. The rate of investment growth fluctuated in sub-Saharan Africa, but the decline was most visible in West Asia and Latin America. In addition, many of the "tigers" in the South Asia region also seem to suffer from a decelerating pattern of investment expenditure.

Deceleration of fixed investment expenditure was, not surprisingly, a factor that explained one of the greatest enigmas of current times: an overall decrease in the rate of productivity. The second and third sets of columns in Table 2.3 report the average labor productivity, and Figs. 2.6 and 2.7A–B show total factor productivity (TFP) growth rates across selected countries. Labor productivity, particularly in the industrial sectors, was negative in many countries during the great recession, and seems to be persisting into the 3rd decade of the 21st century. Industrial labor productivity growth was

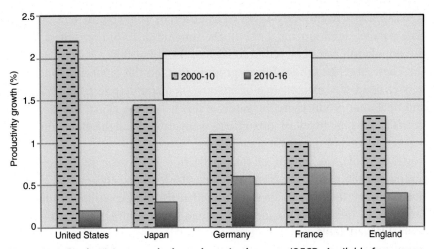

Figure 2.6 *Productivity growth slows down in the core. (OECD, Available from: www. data.oecd.org).*

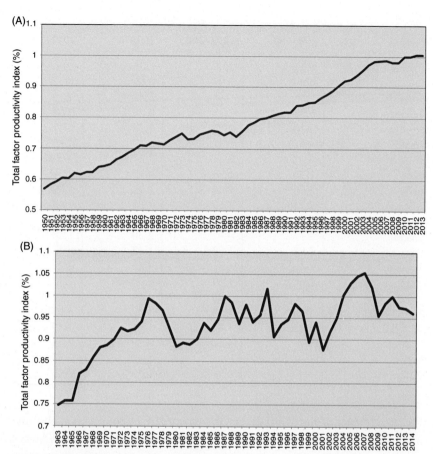

Figure 2.7 *(A) USA total factor productivity index (2011=1.00). (B) Turkey: total factor productivity index (2011=1.00). (University of Groningen, Penn World Table, v. 9.0).*

reported as zero in Latin America, while East Asia showed sustained, and yet volatile, rates of growth.

A comparison of TFP between the 1st decade of the 21st century and the early 2010s shows that the deceleration was significant in many developed countries (Fig. 2.6). The productivity growth gap between the 1st and 2nd decade was most visible in the United States and Japan, and although Germany and France seemed to have achieved some progress, their performances were still below their respective historical averages.

Comparisons across longer time periods also revealed similar observations. Data in Table 2.4, and Fig. 2.7 illustrate that the declining productivity growth rates were the cause of the great recession in the post-2010 period. Table 2.4 indicates that the slowdown in the rate of productivity

Table 2.4 Rate of productivity growth (values expressed as percentages)

	1981–90	1991–2000	2003–08	2011–14
Austria	1.11	2.09	0.76	2.06
Canada	0.89	1.85	0.69	1.12
Czech Republic	—	—	3.88	0.39
France	3.01	2.15	0.78	0.64
Germany	2.38	2.05	1.22	0.51
Greece	—	1.41	1.10	0.15
Hungary	—	2.74	3.31	−0.32
Italy	1.90	1.73	0.17	0.06
Japan	4.05	1.96	1.25	0.59
Korea	7.71	5.60	4.60	0.43
Mexico	—	0.22	0.76	0.92
Poland	—	—	2.30	1.48
Portugal	2.07	1.52	1.43	0.47
Slovakia	—	—	4.22	2.21
Spain	2.60	1.04	0.56	1.41
Turkey	3.96	2.29	4.44	−0.03
United Kingdom	1.78	2.58	1.32	−0.09
United States	1.45	1.84	1.41	0.19
Chile	—	4.13	3.89	2.94
Russia	—	—	5.49	1.35
OECD average	—	—	1.33	0.45

was already part of historical reality for most OECD countries at the turn of the century. In comparison to the 1980s, only two countries (Austria and Canada) achieved increased rates of productivity growth. In contrast, Hungary, Turkey, and the United Kingdom had negative productivity gains, while the OECD average fell sharply.

At this juncture it might be useful to refresh our understanding of the historical trends in the rate of productivity growth. Fig. 2.7 documents TFP growth over a longer time period in two case studies: (1) the United States, which is the center of the global economic system; and (2) Turkey, which is the main focus of this study. Penn World Table data from the University of Groningen shows that US TFP had two main surges (in the 1950s and in 1980–2000) and two plateaus of deceleration between these surges (in the 1970s and the current phase). Conversely, TFP growth was both volatile and erratic in Turkey, a typical observation seen in the most emerging economies of the developing world.

These historical observations were carried over to the future projections in the OECDs 2014 policy paper on "Policy Challenges for the Next

50 Years" OECD (2014). The projections stated that the global economy would likely slow from its yearly average of 3.6% during 2014–30 to 2.7% in 2030–60, and the growth rate of the developed world would slow to as little as 0.5% by 2060. It was also estimated that greenhouse gas (GHG) emissions (from industrial processes and fossil fuel combustion) would rise twofold, increasing from 48,700 to 99,500 million tons by 2060. As a consequence, the negative effects of climate change would likely lead to production and income losses of 1.5%–5% across Asia and East Asia.

These observations revealed a vicious circle, whereby a decline in wage incomes and the collapse of middle incomes led to a fall in effective demand and subsequent stagnation. The post-1980 scenario saw profit recovery through financial rent seeking, albeit by diverging saving funds away from fixed investments toward financial rentier activities with cutthroat and damaging speculative bubbles, and through the significant deceleration in productivity gains (Fig. 2.8).

The main aim of this manuscript is to break this vicious circle. In the flowing pages, viable alternative policy scenarios, such as the activation of green employment and green growth development strategies, are suggested to address the problems of duality and segmentation by utilizing the ability of these instruments to combat climate change. A deeper analysis of the

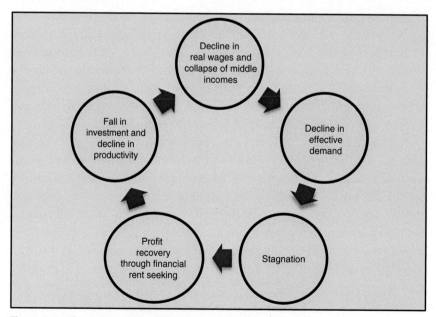

Figure 2.8 *The vicious circle of the 21st century global economy.*

current challenges facing the developing world (i.e., structural transformation, deindustrialization, and duality) are initially discussed.

2.2 DEVELOPMENTAL IMPORTANCE OF STRUCTURAL CHANGE AND INDUSTRIALIZATION

Economic development involves growth and structural change, and economic growth is intrinsically linked to changes in production structure. In its broadest meaning, successful structural transformation is associated with a shift in the share of output and employment from low- (agriculture) to high-productivity activities (Ros, 2000). This has typically meant a decreasing share of agriculture in total value added and employment, and an increasing share of industry and services. This long-term process has been accompanied by a shift in the labor force from rural to urban areas, and the continuous reallocation of employment from agriculture to services and industry.

However, this process is not simple and it does not achieve the final target. "Successful" structural change involves adopting and adapting to existing technologies, diversifying production activities, and upgrading production structures across the economy (Amsden, 2001). Hence the overall process strongly follows the idea of "cumulative causation," which was put forward by Young (1928) and Schumpeter (1939) to explain economic growth and development. The idea was cultivated and structured further for the analysis of structural change (Hirschman, 1958; Kaldor, 1966; Myrdal, 1957)[1] and emphasizes that at the heart of structural change lies the process of "cumulative causation," which reinforces and increases the pace of economic growth. Industrial expansion creates employment, increases incomes and demands, and leads to increased productivity.

Kaldor's framework (Kaldor, 1966, 1967) provides a thorough theoretical basis and a set of empirical regularities that emphasize the dynamics of cumulative causation. The framework emphasizes the central role of industry (specifically manufacturing) by bringing together the notions of "engine of growth" sectors, "economies of scale," and "sectoral shifts" in an informative way. The framework recognizes that manufacturing plays an important role in generating production linkages and pulling the rest of the economy, thus

---

[1] The idea reappears in more recent analyses of industrial take-off (Matsuyama, 1992; Murphy et al., 1989) and in new economic geography literature (Combes et al., 2008; Harris, 1954; Krugman, 1991).

producing productivity gains through dynamic economies of scale. High-productivity gains in manufacturing create technological externalities to the rest of the economy. Thus Kaldor derived conditions that linked growth output, employment growth, and productivity within and among different sectors of the economy, which are now known as Kaldor's growth laws[2].

Broadly speaking, Kaldor's Growth Laws emphasize that industrialization is critical to both faster economic growth and structural transformation. The main argument of the laws is that there is a strong causal relationship between the growth of manufacturing output and the growth of manufacturing productivity. This is based on the characteristics of industry, which offer special prospects for capital accumulation and the acquisition of new technologies, and provide greater opportunities for dynamic economies of scale. Manufacturing growth not only has spillover effects on other sectors but is also associated with the reallocation of resources and employment from other sectors (normally with lower productivity levels), therefore aggregate productivity growth of the economy is positively associated with the growth of manufacturing output and employment[3]. Thus manufacturing tends to have a greater impact on aggregate output and productivity[4].

The composition of demand will progressively turn toward services, a sector that will incorporate a growing share of the work force due to its slower gains in productivity. The classic structural transformation in the economy described by Kuznets (1973) therefore involves a shift from agriculture to nonagriculture and subsequently from industry to services.

---

[2] Kaldor's laws, as a set of empirical regularities emphasizing the sectoral composition of output and interallocation of labor from low- to high-growth sectors and the dynamics of productivity, may also be considered to set the foreground for (endogenous) growth models that do not rely on diminishing returns to capital and that recognize sectoral differentiation.

[3] Kaldor focuses on productivity gains for the overall economy to highlight that it is not only important that resources are reallocated from low- to high-productivity (manufacturing) activities to increase average productivity levels (the notion of temporary structural bonus, Baumol et al., 1985, 1989), but rather that this must raise the average productivity growth over time (the notion of dynamic structural change bonus).

[4] Such effects spread to the whole economy and lead to "cumulative causation" through a variety of linkages. Manufacturing has the strongest Hirschmanian-type (Hirschman, 1958) backward (expanding demand for its inputs) and forward (expanded production possibilities for downstream) input–output linkages. Moreover, industry also serves as the focal point of learning linkages through the generation of technology and knowledge spillover. Reallocation effects further reinforce income linkages through Kuznetsian channels of rural–urban migration, and through multiplier effects of changing consumer demand due to higher incomes generated in the "pulling sector" of the economy.

Both supply and demand factors are significant in this process. The demand-based argument follows the shifts in consumption structure as countries move toward higher levels of per capita income. As per capita income increases, the share of agriculture initially decreases due to low-income elasticity of demand for its products, and thus the share of manufactured goods increases (Engel's Law)[5]. As income growth continues, consumption preferences move from the manufacturing to the services sector. The supply-based explanation follows the argument that industrial manufacturing is the leading sector of technological upgrading, and innovation and productivity growth are generally higher in this sector compared to the other sectors of the economy. Thus rapid productivity growth implies a reduction in the share of manufacturing employment, but not necessarily in the share of value added (Rodrik, 2015).

2.2.1 Myths and Miracles: Trends in Structural Change in Developing Countries

The changes in the sectoral composition of output and employment (relative to GDP per capita) in the period since 1970 largely confirm the dynamics of economic growth described in the previous section; however, there are some very important differences and caveats. Most advanced economies with existing high-income levels saw a reduction in the relative weight of manufacturing output and employment and an increase in the relative weight of services. Complementarities in these economies ensured a steady rise in "modern services" (i.e., transportation, energy, communication, and finance), which were able to produce "decent" jobs in terms of productivity and remuneration. As the economies moved to higher levels of GDP per capita, the shares of agricultural and services employment declined and increased, respectively. Fig. 2.9 depict the shares of developed and developing countries in world manufacturing value added during 1970–2013. In 1970, developing countries accounted for 30% of global industry value added in current USD prices and 19.5% in constant 2005 USD prices. In nominal terms, the increasing trend for the developing economies in the 1970s was followed by a collapse during the 1980s and 1990s (due to the debt crisis and real depreciation of the currencies of developing country), and a recovery with a higher rate of growth in the 2000s. In 2010, developing

---

[5] One implication of this economic-development process is that countries specializing in agriculture-based or commodity-based primary production will eventually face demand obstacles to growth.

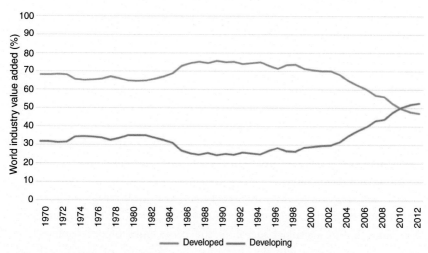

Figure 2.9 *Share in world industry value added (% current $). (UNSD).*

economies had a higher share of global industry value added than advanced economies. In real terms, the share of developing economies continued to increase slightly during 1970–2013, and reached 45% in 2013. Therefore from a low base in 1970 (and from a much lower base when the immediate aftermath of World War II is considered), developing economies have experienced significant increases in industrial production. The distinction between developed and developing countries, in terms of real per capita income and associated sectoral shares of output and employment, is also clear. For industry in general, and the manufacturing sector in particular, there is a point beyond which the shares started to decline.

"Deindustrialization" has generally been associated with the growth of advanced economies, and the term is used to define the secular decline in manufacturing employment, a phenomenon that had already started in the 1960s. Therefore deindustrialization in developed economies is considered a natural result of the shift from manufacturing toward services[6]. Deindustrialization out of economic dynamism assumes that industrialization has already exploited the expansion period and has reached its final stages (Cruz, 2015). It also assumes that the services sector has matured to absorb new workers in high-quality jobs. Deindustrialization in advanced economies generally occurs when industrialization has already raised overall

[6] The early contributions of Baumol (1967), Fuchs (1968), and Rowthorn and Ramaswamy (1997, 1999) provided a framework to analyze the possible explanations (and contributions) of the phenomenon.

productivity, disseminated its technological capacities, and consolidated a domestic market (UNCTAD, 2016).

However, deindustrialization alone is not sufficient to describe the path that many low- and middle-income developing economies have experienced since the 1980s. With some exceptions (largely in Asia), developing economies have also been subject to substantial deindustrialization, especially since the 1980s; however, these countries began at levels of per capita income that were much lower than when advanced economies started to deindustrialize; a phenomenon labeled as "premature deindustrialization."[7]

The spread of industry/manufacturing to developing countries occurred largely during the post-World War II period. Manufacturing has since emerged as a crucial sector in the economies of developing economies, perhaps fundamentally changing the structure of global industrial production and trade. Large quantities of industrial activity and industrial production have moved from advanced to developing countries; some developing economies have displayed periods of rapid catch-up (i.e., East Asian late-industrializing countries), while some have experienced periods of collapsing growth (i.e., Latin America and Africa).

However, the development observed in advanced economies has only partially been replicated in developing countries. These uneven experiences are seen using the indicator of "industrial convergence." Fig. 2.10 displays the manufacturing share of GDP relative to that of the average of advanced G7 countries. The figure shows that there has been a tendency for developing countries to narrow the industrialization gap. This tendency is closely related to the trends and associated positional changes of the developed and developing countries, and it is also a result of the deindustrialization of the advanced economies. Nevertheless, regional differences in the narrowing of the industrialization gap are apparent; for example, Asian countries have not only been successful in closing the gap, but in some cases (East and South East Asia) they have overtaken advanced countries in industrialization. However, the collapse of the manufacturing sector in transition economies, and the limits of the Latin American industrialization process, are also apparent in Fig. 2.10. One of the most striking observations from the figure is that, as of 2010, countries in sub-Saharan Africa have been unable to narrow the industrialization gap with developed economies, and have displayed regression with respect to the variable under concern. Hence the considerable

---

[7] See Palma (2005, 2008), Rodrik (2015), and Tregenna (2009) for further discussions on the driving factors, characterization, and consequences of premature deindustrialization.

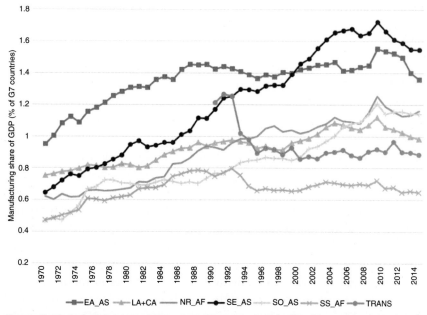

Figure 2.10 *Industrial convergence or divergence using the share of manufacturing in GDP as a percent of that of advanced G7 countries.* EA_AS, East Asia; LA+CA, Latin America and the Caribbean; NR_AF, North Africa; SE_AS, South-east Asia; SO_AS, South Asia; SS_AF, Sub-Saharan Africa; TRANS, Transition Economies. *(UNSD).*

regional unevenness in the industrialization efforts and performances of developing countries in the post-1970 period are emphasized, with Latin America and sub-Saharan Africa experiencing failures and East and South East Asia experiencing major improvements.

On closer inspection, there has been clear decline in the share of output and employment provided by agriculture. However, several middle-income countries, and some least developed countries, have experienced relative declines in their shares of manufacturing output and employment before reaching per capita income levels that were significantly lower than those historically observed in advanced economies. Such tendencies could imply a fundamental break from previous norms, with services replacing (or at least complementing) manufacturing as an engine of economic growth (Dasgupta and Singh, 2005, 2006). However, it could also be argued that this is far from being "a proper experience of industrialization" (Rodrik, 2015), and is rather a process of "killing of the necessary increasing returns sector of the periphery" (Reinert, 2008). Such discussions are also relevant for questions of whether natural resource-based industries, which often depend on static comparative advantage, could significantly contribute as complementary engines of growth (Cimoli and Katz, 2003; Lawrence, 2005; McMillan et al., 2014).

The diversity in the performance of developing economies also points to different relationships between economic growth and structural change (as outlined earlier). Table 2.5 provides data used to obtain a better understanding of the links between growth and structural change in developing regions. For example, the table presents the crucial macroeconomic elements of structural transformation including the GDP growth, share of manufacturing value added, aggregate employment growth, and labor productivity growth.

Two major points that arise instantly are the contrasts between the developing regions, and the contrast between pre- and post-1980 for a number of developing economies. With the exception of East Asia and South Asia (and sub-Saharan Africa post-2000), no developing region was able to maintain the annual GDP growth rates of the 1970s in the proceeding periods. The sharp decrease in GDP growth in Latin America, West Asia, and North Africa in the 1980s was concomitant with a sharp decrease in industry output growth during this time.

However, the regions that experienced reductions in GDP growth post-1980 did not experience an instant parallel decline in employment. Thus the adjustment of low-output growth rates fell onto lower labor productivity growth rates. The average annual productivity growth during the 1980s was −1.9% for Latin America and −0.9% in sub-Saharan Africa.

Such employment-generating dynamics were clearly not sustainable in Latin America, at least not in industry. Thus employment growth in deindustrializing Latin America continued at rates that were comparable to that of industrializing Asia during 1980–2000, only at much lower productivity growth rates and in nonindustry sectors of the economy (i.e., in services and informal sectors, which are often associated with commodity booms). The North African countries in Table 2.5 (i.e., Egypt, Morocco, and Tunisia) and Turkey are examples of economies that tried to maintain some degree of industrialization with little structural changes to sustain productivity growth. The high growth rates seen in these countries in the 1970s has been decreasing, and has often swung abruptly between boom and bust depending on the global economic conditions.

Thus the uneven performances in developing regions lies not in their differing abilities to generate industrial employment or the overall economy, but in their remarkably different capacities to generate and

Table 2.5 Elements of structural transformation

		Developed countries	Latin America and the Caribbean	East Asia	South East Asia	South Asia	Sub-Saharan Africa	North Africa
GDP growth (%)	1970s	4.1	4.5	7.3	7.3	3.0	3.4	6.1
	1980s	2.7	1.4	8.1	5.4	4.7	2.4	4.5
	1990s	1.5	2.6	4.9	4.9	4.8	2.9	3.4
	2000–07	3.4	3.9	7.6	5.1	5.6	4.5	4.5
	2010–14	1.2	3.1	6.6	4.8	5.8	5.4	2.4
Employment growth (%)	1970s	1.0	3.0	3.5	3.6	1.6	3.0	2.8
	1980s	0.9	2.8	2.6	3.0	2.9	3.2	2.2
	1990s	−0.1	2.2	1.5	2.3	2.3	2.2	2.4
	2000–07	1.3	2.6	1.4	2.3	2.8	2.7	3.3
	2010–14	0.3	2.0	1.3	1.6	2.0	3.1	1.6
Labor productivity growth (%)	1970s	3.1	1.7	3.7	3.6	1.3	0.5	3.3
	1980s	1.8	−1.9	5.8	2.4	1.8	−0.9	2.3
	1990s	1.6	1.2	5.0	2.6	2.6	0.2	1.0
	2000–07	2.1	1.1	5.0	2.8	2.8	2.7	1.2
	2010–14	0.8	1.3	4.1	3.2	3.8	2.7	0.8
Manufacturing value-added share (%)	1970s	26.4	21.7	28.3	17.7	16.2	12.7	20.8
	1980s	22.8	20.8	34.9	22.3	19.3	14.8	17.0
	1990s	20.6	21.6	34.2	24.5	20.5	15.6	20.0
	2000–07	16.8	17.5	30.1	26.6	18.9	11.6	18.0
	2010–14	14.7	14.5	29.4	23.1	17.7	9.6	16.7

Source: Compiled from GGDC–10 sector database, UNSD, WDI, KILM, TED.

sustain productivity growth. Most developing regions, with the exception of Asia, have seen an increasing productivity gap relative to advanced economies. Only a few countries have shown the ability to catch up, or at least keep up, with the productivity dynamics of advanced economies, while simultaneously maintaining the dynamics for employment generation (Fig. 2.11A–D).

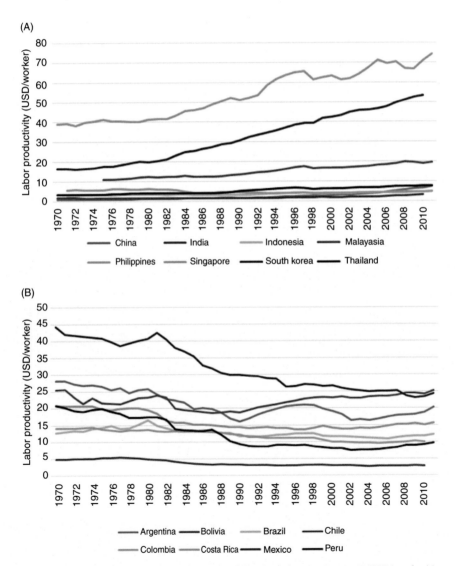

Figure 2.11 *Relative labor productivity (% of developed countries, 2005 USD/worker) in (A) Asia, (B), Latin America, (C) North Africa, and (D) sub-Saharan Africa. (Compiled from GGDC-10 sector database).*

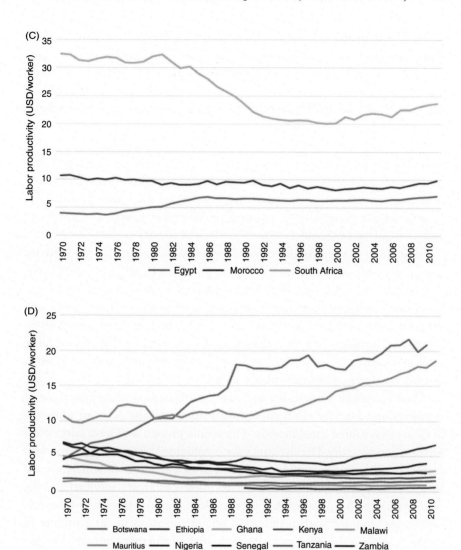

Figure 2.11 (*Continued*).

2.2.2 Potential Consequences of Premature Deindustrialization

Following the argument that industry is crucial for building production and links to sustain aggregate productivity growth, premature deindustrialization would mean a reduced growth potential and reduced possibilities for convergence. Thus premature deindustrialization represents a pathological state as it has the potential to stop the economy from achieving its full growth, employment, and resource utilization potential (Singh, 1977).

In line with the theoretical discussions presented in the previous sections, manufacturing tends to be the most technologically dynamic sector and it exhibits unconditional convergence (Rodrik, 2013). Thus when premature deindustrialization occurs, the manufacturing sector weakens as the engine of growth. The prospect for sustaining aggregate productivity growth is also likely to simultaneously decline, as the economy becomes deprived of the increasing returns-to-scale sector that provides the necessary environment to achieve technological progress, skill acquisition, and institutional deepening. As the ability to generate sustained productivity growth is crucial for achieving structural transformation, stagnating productivity growth would eventually be associated with lower capital accumulation, employment, and income.

Slowdown in the economic growth rate leads to aggregate productivity stagnation, which coupled with declining investments, generates insufficient jobs and lower quality jobs. With a large surplus of labor in agricultural and other primary services, and with informal economies of considerable size, premature deindustrialization and lack of structural transformation place immense constraints on developing countries dynamically transforming their economies (i.e., with output, employment, and productivity growth) toward long-term development objectives.

Slow economic growth is associated with increased underutilization of resources, and a lack of structural transformation will also act as an additional factor in resource misallocation. The whole process will have adverse effects on productivity. The dynamics for employment generation in modern sectors of the economy will be weak, and in such an environment, labor will be absorbed by low-productivity sectors (mostly auxiliary services) and the informal sector (i.e., low-quality jobs and low wages). These dual-economy conditions, coupled with reallocation effects and shifts in the structure of production, would further contribute to slow productivity growth. The apparent differences in productivity between sectors implies substantial losses in aggregate productivity. High unemployment and flexible labor markets put no pressure on wages and create no incentive for further investment to stimulate productivity growth. Thus slow economic performance and slow productivity growth create the basis for the growing (cyclical) underutilization of resources that characterize a low-growth environment, reflecting the conditions for reverse causality to take action and leaving a narrow space for any structural transformation to come about.

After a successful period of growth and development from the 1950s, the post-1980 period for many developing countries was characterized by export-led growth strategies based on liberalization of the commodity and financial markets. In the context of export-led growth and liberalized trade, premature deindustrialization creates further challenges for successful transformation. Under such conditions, investments and domestic linkages to substitute imported capital goods are severely hindered, if not fully restrained. Thus the country may become an exporter of (even manufactured) goods, mainly produced by imported capital goods and inputs. Therefore the (tradable) manufacturing sector would be deprived of all backward and forward linkages, reducing its potential to pull along the economy. Hence export-led growth cannot generate dynamics of sustained growth for the overall economy (Cruz, 2015).

Building upon such foundations, a broader perspective on structural change and growth emphasizes the growth and export performance of modern sectors of the economy. It stresses the importance of constantly generating new activities as well as the ability of these activities to absorb surplus labor and promote integration with domestic sectors of the economy (Ocampo, 2008). Industry tends to have a greater potential for inducing deeper domestic integration. Domestic linkages not only trace the whole production process from raw materials to semifinished products, but they also trace to other sectors of the economy including modern services of transportation and communication and ancillary services. The degree of domestic integration of the economy further influences the ability of the domestic market to contribute to high and sustained growth.

2.3 DUALITY IN ECONOMIC THEORY: A SUMMARY AND IMPLICATIONS

The narrative used to describe the consequences of premature deindustrialization in developing countries, in effect, illustrates the framework to comprehend the relationship between structural transformation and economic growth. In developing economies, structural transformation is a multidimensional phenomenon that requires adopting and adapting to technologies, rapidly accumulating physical and human capital, substituting imports, and entering manufactured goods and services into world markets (Ocampo, 2008). Therefore analyzing the experiences of different developing regions and countries is important to understand the nature of relationships between growth and structural change.

UNCTAD (2003) effectively outlined the process of structural transformation that leads to sustained productivity and economic growth.

The accumulation of capital leads to the employment of surplus labor and the use of underutilized resources in the production process, which is key to raising capita income and living standards in an economy. It is a crucial variable for growth and structural change as it simultaneously allows the expansion of production capacity and effective demand, and it also carries strong complementarities with other elements that determine long-term growth. Long-term economic success depends on sustained improvements in productivity via the acquisition of skills and technological progress. Thus each worker producing more from a given level of effort provides the basis for rising incomes and living standards. Therefore it is productivity gains, and not simply additional employment, that characterizes accumulation and growth. Such a process is invariably associated with structural changes in output and employment. This occurs through shifts in economic activities across agriculture, industry, and services, and through upgrading to higher value-added activities within each sector with the introduction of new products and processes. The importance of structure to the development process is partly due to the fact that the overall level of income is closely related to the allocation of resources among sectors.

One theoretical alternative that contributes to our understanding of the causal relationships between structural transformation and economic growth embodies the notion of the "dual economy," which has been built on contributions by Boeke (1953), Chenery and Syrquin (1975), Higgins (1956), Jorgenson (1961, 1966, 1967), Lewis (1954), and Ranis and Fei (1961). The dual-economy model served as one of the basic models of development theory for several decades after World War II, and it is also the basis of a vast amount of literature in development economics. Scholars including Mundlak (2000), Ros (2000); Temple (2005a,b); and Vollrath (2009a,b)[8], emphasize the importance of considering and representing the interdependencies of different sectors, subsistence wages, patterns of unemployment and underemployment, labor market imperfections, and savings, and allowing explicitly for the possibility of (qualitatively) different types of growth.

Based on the conceptualization by Lewis (1954), the theory proposes a "dual structure" for developing countries, where two (or multiple) economies with fundamentally different structures coexist and interact in a country. One economy is usually regarded as the traditional sector, which is

---

[8] Gollin (2014); Lombardo (2012); Rangazas and Mourmouras (2013); and Temple (2005a) provide thorough overviews on dual economies and growth.

characterized by a stagnant backward structure that relies on elementary production technologies, unskilled labor, and natural resources. The other economy is represented as the modern sector, and utilizes advanced capital-intensive technologies and skilled labor. The interdependence among the economy sectors (which exhibit different asymmetric structures in terms of their productivity, labor and capital markets) and household saving and consumption behavior often leads to multiple qualitatively different equilibria, which leaves ample room for policy intervention. Hence the theory allows the analysis of factor misallocation, urban unemployment, migration, informality, and international variations in productivity, and hence the interaction between growth and structural change.

In its basic form, the "dual-economy model" supposes a small open economy with two sectors and two factors of production. The traditional (agricultural) sector contains an abundant endowment of (unskilled) labor working with very low (near zero) productivity and for subsistence wage. Conversely, the modern (industrial) sector employs labor at a rate that is higher than the subsistence wage provided in the traditional sector. The "transfer" of surplus labor from the traditional sector to the modern sector affects aggregate labor productivity. It also contributes to the development of the modern sector by producing an investment fund financed by the surplus production in the traditional sector (Jorgenson, 1961; Ranis and Fei, 1961; Ruttan, 1968). Thus the model provides the basis for understanding: (1) the conditions for the breakdown of economic transformation that leads to sustained growth; (2) the characterization of the "turning point" at which the economy ceases to be "underdeveloped"; and (3) the implications of technological change in agriculture (i.e., how innovations under the Green Revolution affect agricultural technology and productivity).

"Modern sector dualism" (Bertrand and Squire, 1980) uses the basic ideas of the traditional dual-economy models, but focuses more on labor market imperfections or market imperfections (which carry effects onto the labor markets). When wages or marginal products of labor are not equalized among the sectors of the economy, the aggregate TFP and dynamics of economic growth will inevitably be influenced by reallocation of labor from one sector to another. Wage differentials have been linked to spatial separation between traditional (rural) and modern (urban) sectors of the economy, therefore the "duality" framework can be further developed to study and understand the dynamics of urbanization and urban unemployment. Work by Harris and Todaro (1970), and the open economy version developed by Corden and Findlay (1975), provide the basis for analyzing informality (urban unemployment) and the general equilibrium implications of rural–urban migration. More recent studies that have used dual-economy models to study the dynamics of informality, urbanization, and the relationship between urbanization and economic growth include Banerjee and Newman (1993), Henderson (2010), Rauch (1993), and Yuki (2007).

The framework is especially relevant for studying the effects of economic dualism on income inequality and poverty (Bourguignon, 1990; Bourguignon and Morrisson, 1998; Temple, 2005b; Yuki, 2007). Deriving the conditions when economic growth becomes conducive for an egalitarian distribution of income, and how the share of the traditional sector in the economy interacts with these conditions, becomes especially important in the context of structural change and deindustrialization.

If the two sectors were also associated with geographical differences (i.e., the modern sectors are urban and the traditional sectors are rural), households living and producing in different regions may also show behavioral differences. Such differences would be visible in the households' decision to save, invest in education and human capital, and reproduce. This would therefore have important consequences on the dynamics of productivity and growth (Das et al., 2015; Masson, 2001; Rangazas and Mourmouras, 2013).

Finally, the duality framework can also be extended to study the interactions between environmental policies and economic growth. De Oliveira and Lima (2015) analyzed the dual relationship between pollution abatement policies (which affect modern sectors of the economy) and environmental quality affecting labor productivity. Their analysis shed light on the impact of environmental policies on profitability in the modern sector, savings, productivity, and growth dynamics. Furthermore, the conditions under which the country is led to an "ecological development trap" (i.e. the presence of a pollution abatement mechanism that operates when the current level of environmental quality is below its maximum attainable level) can also be analyzed.

2.4 MACROECONOMICS OF THE ENVIRONMENT

Existing evidence on the global economy suggests that growth over the next century is likely to be erratic and highly uneven. For example, an OECD (2014) report claims that the world economy will significantly slow down during the next 50 years. OECD researchers argue that this prognostication rests on two important factors: (1) the duality and unevenness of income distribution across functional and regional sense, with a consequent rise in social exclusion and conflict; and (2) environmental pollution due to the threat of climate change. This section deals with the implications of economic growth in a dualistic manner for sustainability, resource use, environment, and climate change.

2.4.1 Sustainability, Resource Use, and the Environment in a Dual World

Extensive research, particularly since the beginning of the 1970s, has focused on the relationship between economic growth, the utilization of natural resources, and the changes in environmental quality. Studies have suggested that Earth has exceeded its ecological boundaries, especially since the Industrial Revolution (Hahnel, 2010). This is easily demonstrated by the ecological footprint indicator, which shows the geographical area required by human beings to meet the natural resource needs of various economic activities, which serve consumption at the end. Data from the Global Footprint Network in 2010 stated that Earth cannot supply in 1 year the amount of natural resources warranted by our current annual consumption level, and consequently the stock of natural resources are rapidly declining. The authors observed that by 2010, 102 out of 139 countries had produced greater consumption footprints than their own biocapacities. It is possible for countries to consume more than the regeneration capacity of their own resources only if they import resources from other countries, otherwise their natural resource stocks would deplete. It is clear that none of these paths are sustainable in the long run. Moreover, the fact that some countries meet the deficit between their consumption levels and their biocapacities through imports cannot be ignored, as this exacerbates global inequalities in natural resource use and will have adverse social implications on a global level.

The first international document to introduce the concept of sustainability was a report entitled "World Conservation Strategy," which was published in 1980 by the IUCN, UNEP, and WWF (IUCN, 1980). In this report, sustainable development was defined as a development process that does not restrict posterity's right to access resources. The concept was popularized by the well-known "Our Common Future" report, also known as the Brundtland Report, published by WCED (1987).

Sustainability entails sustained resources. Human activities mainly depend on three types of capital: physical, human, and natural resources. As the literature has grown, the notion of sustainability has been redefined into two categories: "strong" and "weak" sustainability. Weak sustainability asserts that the three main forms of capital are perfect substitutes for one another. According to this view, a country that achieves economic growth through exporting coal or other nonrenewable natural resources (which will deplete) cannot be claimed to be on an unsustainable path. If the country in question has used the revenue it generated from the sale of its irreplaceable natural resources to increase its physical or human capital, this means that its capital has increased in one form while decreasing in another, thus leaving the total capital stock intact. One key factor that leads to weak sustainability is technological advances and innovations; for instance, recycling technologies or products (i.e., synthetic fiber) allow the same levels of demand to be met using fewer natural resources. Conversely, the notion of strong sustainability dismisses most of these assumptions, particularly the "perfect substitution" assumption. According to this concept, a positive change in one type of capital cannot be substituted for a negative change in another. For example, when a decrease in oil stocks occurs due to overconsumption, transference of oil revenue into education, physical capital (i.e., machinery and equipment), or natural capital (i.e., creating new forests) does not mean that the level of total capital stock is kept constant. One problem of weak sustainability is that while the precise monetary value of physical capital can be measured, it is impossible to properly convert human and natural capital into monetary terms. The weak sustainability approach merely regards forests as sources of fuel and raw materials for various industries. The only fully-measurable element here is the economic value of wood, which can be traded on the market. From an ecological perspective, forests are entities that do not only provide wood, but they provide various services to different species and play a part in significant cycles (i.e., water and nitrogen cycles). Although it is possible to quantify the ecosystem services that forests provide using certain valuation methods, these estimates will prove to be deficient since they exclude services that have not yet been specified in a scientific manner. Therefore according to the principle of strong sustainability, natural resources cannot be perfectly substituted for physical capital. The conservation and enhancement of natural resources are necessary processes for the perpetuation of human beings, and therefore also constitute the main conditions for the sustainability of economic activities. Deficiencies in identifying ecosystem services have brought forth a principle called the "precautionary principle." Adopted by the strong sustainability approach, this principle states that if the possible future effects of an activity (e.g., producing food and feed products from genetically modified organisms) cannot be fully identified, this activity should not be undertaken.

Economic growth is generated by the integration of three main types of capital (physical, natural, and human) using technology. Sustainability of economic growth implies that the growth path should not diminish the amount of these three forms of capital. Environmental sustainability means that the pressure and destruction inflicted by economic growth on nature (which is measurable by the ecological footprint) should be equal to or less than nature's regeneration capacity (biocapacity). This can be achieved in two ways: (1) by transforming production and consumption patterns using various incentives and regulations, or (2) by substituting artificial products for natural ones through technology and innovation, or benefiting to a greater extent from existing natural resources by enhancing the efficiency. Both of these sustainability measures depend on human and physical capital stock, as well as on institutional structure. In other words, an economic growth path under a certain institutional and political frame may increase the pressure on nature, while the same growth path under a different frame may alleviate such pressure. Although the attributes of the growth path depend heavily on structural and geographical factors as comparative advantages (i.e., being rich in natural resources and having suitable soil and climate conditions), it cannot be claimed that the adopted policies and institutional factors do not matter. For this reason, comparative advantages are observed as dynamic processes, contrary to their static depiction on theoretical grounds.

The pressure on nature takes many forms including the depletion of renewable (i.e., fish stocks) or nonrenewable (i.e., oil) resources, increased levels of solid wastes, increased GHG emissions leading to climate change, loss of ecosystem services, and the deterioration of land use. The first substantial impact of human activity on nature took place with the transition to settled agriculture, and the second boom resulted from the Industrial Revolution (WorldWatch Institute, 2015). However, the question of the economic growth impact on nature (environmental quality) has only occupied economists' agendas since the end of the 1960s. The relationship between growth and the environment has been investigated in many different schools over the years. One group that studies mainstream "environmental economics" argued that the negative effects of growth on nature stemmed from lack of markets, and suggested that nature be made subject to market mechanisms just like manufactured goods. The mainstream "interventionist" school claimed that a social optimum should be reached by means of taxation and regulation, basing their arguments on the assumption that negative effects (negative externalities) are indicators of market failure. Conversely, "political ecology," an approach that is outside the mainstream, renounces the view that nature is a natural resource reserve and asserts that confining the issue to lack of markets, the existence of market distortions, or failure may obscure the power relationships among actors. According to this standpoint, nature has inherent rights and it is not adequate to commodify it or subject it to the same procedures as other human-made raw materials, intermediate goods, or products.

The roles attributed to economic growth in mainstream economic thoughts are not confined to the economic sphere; for example, it is widely anticipated that economic growth will bring about solutions to social and ecological problems as well. In the literature regarding the impact of growth on the environment (environmental quality), one of the most prevalent hypotheses states that environmental pollution increases with economic growth at low-income levels. Thus pollution is expected to diminish when a certain income level is reached. This indicates the presence of an inverted U-shaped relationship between income and environmental pollution, and the resultant curve is called the environmental Kuznets curve (EKC). This hypothesis rests on the application, in the realm of environment, of the relationship between income distribution inequality and per capita income, identified by Kuznets in the 1950s. A standard EKC analysis estimates the impact of a selected per capita income indicator (and its square) on a selected environmental pollution indicator (e.g., GHG emissions) using a regression equation. The EKC hypothesis claims that growth will have a negative impact on environmental quality until a per capita income threshold is reached; however, further income growth will improve environmental quality thereafter. This relationship materializes through three channels: scale, composition, and technology. A rise in per capita national income will lead to a corresponding growth in the population and consumption. When the scale increases, the pressure on nature will follow suit. However, these factors will also cause the income threshold to be exceeded after a while, after which access to cleaner technologies will become easier and this technological transformation will alleviate the pressure on nature. Consequently, when income growth exceeds a certain threshold, production will shift toward cleaner sectors as societal environmental awareness improves. This denotes the composition channel, which functions to relieve the pressure on nature. The implications of these theoretical anticipations is that low- and middle-income countries could continue to grow without having to take into account the degradation of nature, as environmental quality will automatically increase after a certain income level is reached. However, the crucial point is the determination of this threshold. Furthermore, actual data may not conform to the inverted U-shaped curve that is theoretically expected to depict environmental pollution. Therefore the anticipation that economic growth will automatically solve social issues (i.e., income inequality) or ecological problems (i.e., devastation of nature) after a certain amount of time may prove overoptimistic, and it should be tested against the most holistic indicators possible.

Another point is that the environmental policies developed to cope with the negative externalities of economic activity are often designed and evaluated at the national level although they usually have regional impacts. Hence an approach that considers the direct regional consequences of environmental policies (as well as energy policies) may help to address the dual character of growth in developing countries. In addition, there is also a need to reevaluate the concept of green growth from a regional perspective if the focus is to be on the spatial implications of sustained growth.

2.4.2 Literature Findings on the Income–Environment Relationship

The World Wildlife Fund for Nature (WWF, 2012) identified 1975 as the year in which consumption generated an ecological footprint that exceeded the Earth's biological capacity. It was also the time when environmental pollution and the rapid depletion of nonrenewable natural resources, which stemmed from economic activities including production and consumption and are referred to as "negative externalities" in the economics literature, came to occupy a more critical place on economists' agendas.

The beginning of the 1970s saw the development of a formulation called IPAT. The end result of the exchange of opinions between Commoner, Ehrlich, and Holdren, this formulation encapsulates the effects of human activity on the environment (Commoner et al., 1971; Ehrlich and Holden, 1971). In this formulation, "I" stands for impact, "P" for population, "A" for affluence (defined as per capita income), and "T" for technology. Work from Malthus had previously shown that population growth will reach the limits of natural resources for a given level of technology in a short time span. Commoner et al. (1971) stated that affluence, the level of technology, and population growth all impinge upon the environment. He advocated that, even if the population remained stable, affluence-induced consumption would have adverse effects on the environment, and the negative effects arising from high population growth and affluence could be mitigated (to a certain extent) using more environmentally-friendly technologies.

The first prominent reaction against the notion that natural resources could be exploited limitlessly for the sake of economic growth came in a report entitled "The Limits to Growth," which was authored by well-respected scientists within the Club of Rome in 1972 (Meadows et al., 1972). "World models," which were developed using the system dynamics method, asked questions regarding the "sustainability" of economic activities, as they revealed that economic growth could not continue forever and the limits of natural resources would be reached at some point. The term "sustainability" was first introduced in the "Earth Protection Strategy" report in 1980 (IUCN, 1980); however, the concept was popularized in 1987 by the "Our Common Future" report, also known as the Brundtland Report (WCED, 1987).

Sustainability rests on three main pillars; economic, social, and ecological sustainability. Economic sustainability entails maintaining the means of production (physical capital) that ensure material well-being; social sustainability involves maintaining human capital; and ecological sustainability calls for the preservation of natural resource stocks and the restriction of environmental pollution.

The development of indicators to measure the level of sustainability became one of the main objectives of Agenda 21, which was adopted by the United Nations in 1992. Indicators that assess the impact of economic activities on nature from different perspectives do exist (for a detailed analysis see Singh et al., 2012); some of these indicators are one-dimensional (e.g., CO_2 emissions), while others involve different dimensions, such as deforestation, fish stock depletion, and natural resource consumption.

The impact of income growth (economic growth) on the environment continues to be explored in two different streams: the first stream analyzes the income–environment relationship using individual variables (i.e., air pollution, CO_2, SO_2 emission levels, or waste amount), and the second stream uses composite indicators that are obtained by aggregating numerous different variables, and is thus a more holistic approach. Adjusted Net Savings (ANS) published by the World Bank (Hamilton and Clemens, 1999), and the Ecological Footprint published by Global Footprint Network (Rees, 1992), are examples of indicators.

According to the EKC hypothesis, the effects of income variations on the environment occur through different channels. Grossman and Krueger (1991) were the first scholars to introduce the EKC studies, and defined these channels as scale, composition, and technique effects. An increase in the production volume (scale) intensifies the pressure on natural resources and environmental quality, while a shift in production toward less-polluting sectors due to income growth (i.e., a positive change in the production composition) improves the environmental quality. Finally, efficiency gains driven by technological advances constitute the positive impact of technology on environmental quality. Although production growth is uninterrupted following income increases, beyond a certain income threshold difficulties from scale are expected to be eased down or even gradually eliminated with the help of composition and technique effects. Since the beginning of the 1990s, the notion of EKC has led researchers to assume that every economy should focus on its own growth, and that environmental problems will be eliminated alongside economic growth (Kaika and Zervas, 2013).

A standard EKC analysis estimates the impact of per capita income, its square, and its cube (in some studies) on a selected environmental quality indicator (e.g., the quantity of CO_2 eq. GHG emissions) using a regression equation. Although different studies may select different emission types, early studies particularly focused on SO_2 emissions. Analyzing the possible environmental impact of NAFTA, Grossman and Krueger (1991) were the first to discover an EKC relationship between per capita income and SO_2 emissions and suspended particulate matter. Other scholars also attempted to uncover the nature of the relationship between income and environmental quality using individual indicators. Boulatoff and Jenkins (2010) exclusively selected CO_2 and SO_2 quantities in the atmosphere as their environmental quality indicator, Ehrhardt-Martinez et al. (2002) used deforestation, while Grossman and Krueger (1995) used heavy-metal pollution. Other scholars also conducted research on this topic by selecting different geographical regions and different emission and pollution variables. Some of these studies verified the EKC hypothesis (Kaufmann et al., 1998; Shafik and Bandyopadhyay, 1992; Stern and Common, 2001) while others identified contradicting results (Akbostancı et al., 2009).

The EKC literature may be criticized in two ways. First, the relationship between income and environmental quality does not lend itself to be quantified or generalized using a single indicator (i.e., CO_2 or CO_2 eq. emissions). Consumption growth driven by income growth has numerous multidimensional repercussions, including air pollution, deforestation, depletion of fish stocks, and depletion of agricultural land. Therefore employing aggregate, rather than individual, environmental quality indicators (i.e., ANS or the Ecological Footprint) may provide more holistic results.

The second criticism relates to the geographical areas where indicators are measured. As seen in the aforementioned studies, indicators are based on "domestic production or consumption." The levels of water pollution and deforestation, as well as the impact of income growth on environmental quality and natural resource consumption, that are caused by domestic production or consumption can only be measured using indicators at a domestic level. However, income growth not only leads to increased demand for domestic products but also for increases the demand for foreign goods imported for domestic consumption.

The abatement of domestic water pollution or deforestation beyond a certain income threshold may not produce a transition to a more ecologically-sustainable way of life. As countries become wealthier they may prefer to export their natural resource-intensive polluting industries (i.e., paper, cement, and iron–steel industries) and import finished goods. This would enable them to improve their environmental quality and relieve the pressure on natural resources within their respective countries. There are some studies that have drawn attention to this situation; for instance, Wang et al. (2013) concluded that the ecological footprint related to domestic consumption or production, was affected by the consumption and production of ecological footprints, income levels, and biological capacities of neighboring countries. Wiedman (2009) performed a comprehensive assessment of studies that had explored the degree to which international trade impacted on pollution within the context of producer–consumer responsibility. They observed that the recently-growing foreign direct investments (FDI) were mostly in the form of shifting energy and natural resource-intensive polluting industries from developed to developing and less-developed countries (Poelhekke and van der Ploeg, 2012). Lau et al. (2014) also observed that increased FDI and trade openness led to diminished environmental quality. As countries that transform their production composition and concentrate on cleaner industries become wealthier, they export their polluting industries abroad, which in turn enhances their domestic environmental quality. However, no reduction in total global pollution or natural destruction has been observed; in fact, in countries where environmental standards are lower, each unit of production exerts more pressure on the environment. This situation was analyzed within the framework of the "pollution haven" and "race to the bottom" hypotheses (Ayres, 1996; Daly, 1993; Eskeland and Harrison, 2002; Frankel and Rose, 2005). According to the pollution haven hypothesis, when developing and less-developed countries resort to trade and financial liberalization to accelerate their economic growth, they may be forced to lower their labor and environmental standards to further attract FDI. Similar countries may implement the same strategy to remain competitive, which then triggers a race to the bottom in terms of standards. Therefore while relatively poor countries become havens for polluting industries, the domestic environmental quality in wealthy countries may improve without them altering their unsustainable consumption patterns. Bento and Moutinho (2016) concluded that the comparative advantage yielded by international trade liberalization may prompt changes in countries' trade structures, and that the pollution haven hypothesis prevails. With regard to the income–environment relationship, counter arguments exist against the aforementioned hypotheses. Similar to the contention in the EKC hypothesis (i.e., that the pressure on nature can be alleviated through the channel of technique effects), the so-called "gains from trade" hypothesis envisages that domestic firms may be forced to adopt higher environmental standards and make administrative and technological innovations as a result of increasing openness in foreign trade. This means that trade-driven income growth may reduce the pressure on the environment (Eskeland and Harrison, 2002). Empirical studies that have analyzed the effects of FDI and growing trade on environmental quality have failed to put forward conclusive arguments as to which of these hypotheses should be regarded as valid. The majority of sectoral studies concluded that the "pollution haven" and "race to the bottom" hypotheses are valid for traditional polluting industries, whereas the "gains from trade" hypothesis is applicable to the automotive, telecommunication, and transportation industries (Poelhekke and van der Ploeg, 2012).

The message that the EKC hypothesis conveys to low- and middle-income countries is that they should "keep growing and environmental quality will automatically rise in any case beyond a certain threshold." As mentioned earlier, the EKC relationship has been found to prevail for certain polluters but not for others. GHG emissions in most countries are continuing to rise. If there is no such threshold beyond which GHG emissions will automatically decrease, or if that threshold is beyond reach in the medium and long term, then growth-oriented economic policies should give way to new policies that also accommodate social and ecological constraints.

2.4.3 Climate Change and Economic Growth in the Aftermath of Global Financial Turmoil

While global economic policies continue to focus on maintaining growth, many countries have already begun to experience the adverse impacts of global warming and environmental degradation, which further increases concerns regarding climate change. Amidst the debate on the sustainability of production, trade, and consumption, the global community has failed to give a common and strong response to sustainability concerns over the strong economic development ambitions. On the contrary, as a result of the desire for higher levels of industrialization and consumption, national governments generally insist on prioritizing growth strategies at the expense of nature, thus depleting their renewable and nonrenewable resources in an unsustainable manner.

The 2008 global economic crisis has been referred to by many scientists (including Lipietz, 2012) as the "triple crisis," as economic and social problems (i.e., poverty) went hand in hand with income inequalities and ecological crises (i.e., climate change). This definition also hints at the way out of the crisis. In fact, it was argued that growth policies should also ensure social and ecological sustainability (UNEP, 2009). In the aftermath of the Great Depression of 1929, Keynesian policies (New Deal), which were initially implemented in the United States, were designed to simultaneously resolve the economic and social crises. These policies greatly shaped the set up of economic and political institutions in the following years. Given its depth and extensiveness, it is understandable that the global crisis of 2008 has been referred to as the second Great Depression. However, the 2008 crisis had another aspect that did not apply in the 1929 crisis: an ecological crisis that manifested itself mostly in climate change. Some believe that proposing Keynesian policies, which promote production and consumption patterns seen in 1929, as strategies for the new crisis will further aggravate the ecological crisis. According to this view, "Green New Deal" policies should be implemented. Green growth, green businesses, and the green economy are rapidly gaining depth in the economics literature.

The existence of climate change has been scientifically proven and widely accepted. One Intergovernmental Panel on Climate Change (IPCC) report states that "it is extremely likely that human influence has been the dominant cause of the observed warming since the mid-20th century" (Intergovernmental, 2013). Global GHG emissions from fossil fuels have increased tremendously since 1900; however, the IPCC has stated that CO_2 emissions have increased by around 90% since 1970 (IPCC, 2014). Among the GHG emissions that give rise to global warming (i.e., CO_2, CH_4, N_2O, HFCs, PFCs, SF_6, and NF_3), CO_2 is the primary gas emitted through human activity via the combustion of fossil fuels (i.e., coal, natural gas, and oil), industrial processes, agriculture, waste, and land-use changes. As shown in Fig. 2.12, the percentage change in GHG emissions compared with the

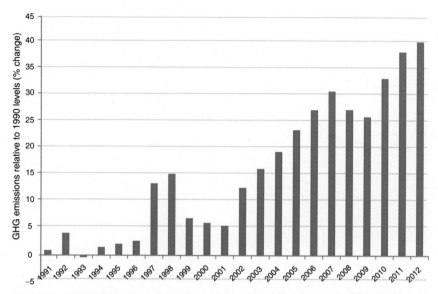

Figure 2.12 *Total GHG emissions (% change from 1990). (World Development Indicators).*

1990 level has been positive throughout 1990–2012, with the exception of 1993 when a mere 0.4% decrease was reported.

The IEA (2012) reported that CO_2 emissions from the energy sector have more than doubled since 1990, and that levels are expected to continue to rise significantly in the medium and long term in line with increasing energy demands. Emissions from coal have been the main global contributor since 2005 and continue to dominate total emissions in a projection to 2040. Coal-related emissions are followed by liquid fuels and by natural gas (Fig. 2.13).

The distribution of global GHG emissions (including land-use change and forestry) is shown in Fig. 2.14. UNFCCC Annex I countries[9], which generally have developed economies, have relatively stable emission levels in comparison to the non-Annex I group of economies. Emission levels from the latter have increased continuously in the last decades, with the top emitters including China, the United States, the European Union, India, the Russian Federation, and Japan (Boden et al., 2017).

[9] Turkey became party to the UNFCCC on May 24, 2004, and ratified the Kyoto Protocol on August 26, 2009. Although it is categorized as a "developing upper-middle income" country according to World Bank classifications, Turkey has "special circumstances" and is listed among the Annex I countries by the UNFCCC.

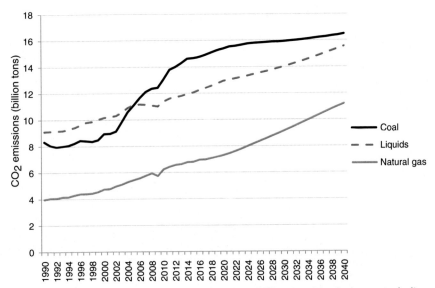

Figure 2.13 *Global energy-related CO$_2$ emissions (billion tons) by fuel type, including projected emissions to 2040. International Energy Outlook 2016 (https://www.eia.gov).*

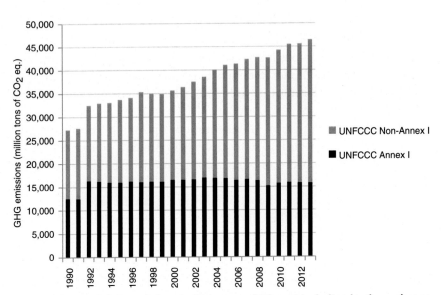

Figure 2.14 *Total GHG emissions (million tons of CO$_2$ eq.) including land-use change and forestry. (WRI/CAIT Climate Data Explorer).*

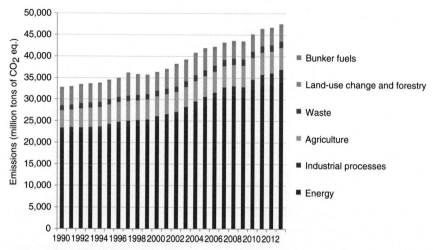

Figure 2.15 *Global GHG emissions by sector (1990–2012). (WRI/CAIT Climate Data Explorer).*

Emissions from the combustion of fossil fuels and industrial processes accounted for the highest share of GHG emissions during 1970–2011 (IPCC, 2014). According to the WRI/CAIT (1985) climate data in Fig. 2.15, the energy sector continued to be the highest contributor to global emissions during 1990–2012.

In addition to the sectors that produce increasing levels of GHG emissions, ongoing energy policies that provide incentives for fossil fuel sectors also proliferate the problem of global warming. One such policy tool is fossil fuel subsidies (FFS). Governments provide FFS to fossil fuel producers or consumers to lower the cost of fossil fuel energy production, increase the price received by energy producers, or decrease the price paid by energy consumers. FFS take many forms, including direct transfers, cross subsidies and price controls to purchase requirements, and tax exemptions (Koplow, 1998). Such subsidies are intended to promote industrialization and lower the price of energy products for consumers; however, FFS have often failed to meet their intended objectives. They are known to impede sustainable development, lead to the economically-inefficient allocation of resources, and accelerate the depletion of natural resources. They cause significant market distortions and act as barriers to energy efficiency and clean energy investments. Most importantly, FFS encourage higher levels of CO_2 emissions, which increase local and global atmospheric pollution.

Table 2.6 Global subsidies on fossil fuels (constant 2015 billion USD)

		2013	2014	2015
Total	**All products**	**493,118**	**459,519**	**321,850**
	Oil	263,504	242,258	144,161
	Electricity	124,578	120,438	100,228
	Natural Gas	103,020	95,201	76,280
	Coal	2,016	1,622	1,181

Source: IEA, 2016. World Energy Outlook, 2016: Fossil Fuel Subsidy Database. Available from: http://www.iea.org/weo/.

Recent IEA data confirmed that fossil fuels (i.e., oil, gas, and coal) receive large chunks of public money in the countries rich in them (Table 2.6). The global value of FFS totaled USD 493, 460, and 322 billion (in 2015 USD) in 2013, 2014, and 2015, respectively. Most of these subsidies were provided within Middle Eastern and North African oil-exporting countries, such as Iran, Kuwait, the United Arab Emirates, Saudi Arabia, Bahrain, Libya, and Algeria (IEA, 2016).

The existence of FFS is a cross-sectoral issue. It does not only apply to energy production or agriculture but also concerns transport services and activities where energy and heat are essential (e.g., industry and housing). FFS can be further divided into producer and consumer subsidies. The OECD estimated that production and consumption subsidies in all G20 countries totaled USD 376 billion in 2014 (Table 2.7). This estimate excludes concessional elements of government support through public finance and state-owned enterprise investment.

Table 2.7 Government support to fossil fuels in G20 countries (USD billion)

	2012	2013	2014
Production	28	21	18
Consumption	398	380	354
Market transfers to consumers	247	236	213
Other transfers (direct payments and tax preferences)	151	144	141
General services	4	6	4

Including subsidies related to the underpricing of electricity.
Source: OECD, 2017. Policies for scaling up low-emission and resilient investment. In: Investing in Climate, Investing in Growth, OECD Publishing, Paris. Available from: http://dx.doi.org/10.1787/9789264273528. Available from: http://www.oecd.org/environment/investing-in-climate-investing-in-growth-9789264273528-en.htm; Table 5.2, p. 196.

In 2009, the G20 leaders committed to "rationalize and phase out over the medium term inefficient FFS that encourage wasteful consumption." This engagement has since been later endorsed by the Asia–Pacific Economic Cooperation. However, solid measures have not yet been taken by the G20 countries. Scientific reports suggest that FFS have the potential to increase the cost of climate change mitigation fivefold or by 20%–25% of a country's GDP (Kovacevic, 2011). In addition, FFS impose heavy burdens on the national balances of payment accounts, especially for the importers of fossil fuels. Eliminating consumer FFS by 2020 could minimize GHGs by 360 million tons, which equates to 12% of the reduction in GHGs needed to hold the global temperature rise at 2°C (IEA, 2013). The IEA estimates that to halve current global carbon emissions and achieve energy sustainability, USD 45 trillion needs to be invested in renewable energy by 2050 (IEA, 2009); however, the continuation of global FFS currently serves as a distorting incentive against renewables.

Energy is essential to all economic activities and to human well-being. Energy services help to meet basic human needs in locations where the lack of access to reliable and affordable modern energy in holding back economies and social development. Energy consumption is fundamental to economic development; however, the current production and use of energy is threatening the global climate, the stability of ecosystems, and the well-being of current and future generations. The introduction of renewable energy would provide an opportunity to phase out some fossil fuels while maintaining appropriate security of the supply.

Current levels of investment in renewable energy are still below their actual potentials. Table 2.8 shows that alternative energy sources (i.e., biomass,

Table 2.8 Potential of renewables (EJ/year)[a]

Resource	Current[b]	Technical	Theoretical potential
Hydropower	9	50	147
Biomass	50	>276	2,900
Solar energy	0.1	>1,575	3,900,000
Wind energy	0.12	640	6,000
Geothermal	0.6	5,000	140,000,000
Ocean energy	NE	NE	7,400
Total	56	>7,600	>144,000,000

NE, Not estimated.
a 1 EJ = 10^{18} joules.
b The electricity part of current use is converted to primary energy with an average factor of 0.385.
Source: World Energy Assessment (UNDP, 2000).

solar, wind, and geothermal power) have tremendous potentials, although only negligible portions of these technical and theoretical potentials are currently being utilized. In addition, renewables are generally more evenly distributed around the globe in comparison to fossil fuels.

Barriers to the implementation of renewable energy include the risks associated with investments (i.e., fiscal policy distortions); the costs of renewable energy projects; and infrastructure, regulatory, market, and financing barriers. A number of steps need to be taken to motivate clean, sustainable, and efficient investment in renewables. These include introducing new technologies; adopting adequate and transparent legal, regulatory, and institutional frameworks; and implementing nondistortionary energy policies (i.e., removing FFS).

2.4.4 The Way Ahead: Global Climate Change Architecture After Paris

Global action has become a must to cope with climate change so that all regions of the world might mitigate the effects of global warming. The need to "cool down" the earth necessitates that various measures be taken, among which is the "substantial and sustained reduction of GHG emissions" (Intergovernmental, 2013). The Paris Agreement, adopted during the 21st Conference of Parties in Paris in December 2015, entered into force on November 4, 2016. This agreement was an unprecedented step toward climate change mitigation on a global scale. The Paris Agreement takes a different approach than the Kyoto Protocol. Instead of setting a quantitative global target for GHG emissions to be met collectively met by parties, the Paris Agreement aims to limit global warming to below a certain level. The most significant feature of this new era is the stipulation that all state parties, both developed and developing, take measures to reduce emissions in accordance with the principle of "common but differentiated responsibilities and respective capabilities" as stated on the United Nations Framework Convention on Climate Change. Within this framework, all states take part in global efforts to fight climate change through the setting of reduction targets calculated by various methods. Therefore both developed and developing countries have reduction responsibilities that are of a similar vein but with different weights. The goals of keeping global warming below 2°C, and intensifying the efforts to limit it to 1.5°C, as set by the Paris Agreement, place a collective responsibility on all countries.

REFERENCES

Akbostancı, E., Türüt-Aşık, S., Tunç, G.İ., 2009. The relationship between income and environment in Turkey: is there an environmental Kuznets curve? Energy Policy 37 (3), 861–867.

Amsden, A., 2001. The Rise of "the Rest": Challenges to the West from Late-Industrializing Economies. Oxford University Press, Oxford, United Kingdom.

Ayres, R., 1996. Limits to the growth paradigm. Ecol. Econ. 19, 117–134.

Banerjee, A.V., Newman, A.F., 1993. Occupational choice and the process of development. J. Polit. Econ. 101 (2), 274–298.

Baumol, W.J., 1967. Macroeconomics of unbalanced growth: the anatomy of urban crisis. Am. Econ. Rev. 57, 415–426.

Baumol, W., Blackman, S.A., Wolff, E.N., 1985. Unbalanced growth revisited: asymptotic stagnancy and new evidence. Am. Econ. Rev. 75 (4), 806–817.

Baumol, W., Blackman, S.A., Wolff, E.N., 1989. Productivity and American Leadership. The Long View. MIT Press, Cambridge, MA.

Bento, J.P.C., Moutinho, V., 2016. CO_2 emissions, non-renewable and renewable electricity production, economic growth, and international trade in Italy. Renew. Sust. Energ. Rev. 55, 142–155.

Bertrand, T., Squire, L., 1980. The relevance of the dual economy model: a case-study of Thailand. Oxf. Econ. Pap. 32 (3), 480–511.

Boden, T.A., Marland, G., Andres, R.J., 2017. National CO_2 emissions from fossil-fuel burning, cement manufacture, and gas flaring: 1751–2014. Carbon Dioxide. Information Analysis Center. United States, Department of Energy, Oak Ridge National Laboratory.

Boeke, J.H., 1953. Economics and Economic Policy of Dual Societies. New York.

Boulatoff, C., Jenkins, M., 2010. Long-term nexus between openness, income, and environmental quality. Int. Adv. Econ. Res. 16, 410–418.

Bourguignon, F., 1990. Growth and inequality in the dual model of development: the role of demand factors. Rev. Econ. Stud. 57 (2), 215–228.

Bourguignon, F., Morrisson, C., 1998. Inequality and development: the role of dualism. J. Dev. Econ. 57, 233–257.

Chenery, H., Syrquin, M., 1975. Patterns of Development 1950–1970. Oxford University Press, London, United Kingdom.

Cimoli, M., Katz, J., 2003. Structural reforms, technological gaps and economic development: a Latin American perspective. Ind. Corp. Change 12 (2), 387–411.

Combes, P., Mayer, T., Thisse, J., 2008. Economic geography. The Integration of Regions and Nations. Princeton University Press, London, United Kingdom.

Commoner, B., Corr, M., Stamler, P.J., 1971. The causes of pollution. Environ. Sci. Policy 3, 2–19.

Corden, W.M., Findlay, R., 1975. Urban unemployment intersectoral capital mobility and development policy. Economica 42, 59–78.

Cruz, M., 2015. Premature de-industrialisation: theory, evidence and policy recommendations in the Mexican case. Camb. J. Econ. 39 (1), 113–137.

Daly, H.E., 1993. The perils of free trade. Sci. Am. Mag. 269 (5), 24–29.

Das, S., Mourmouras, A., Rangazas, P.C., 2015. Economic Growth and Development: A Dynamic Dual Economy Approach. Springer, New York.

Dasgupta, S., Singh, A., 2005. Will services be the new engine of Indian economic growth? Dev. Change 36 (6), 1035–1058.

Dasgupta, S., Singh, A., 2006. Manufacturing, services and premature deindustrialization in developing countries: a Kaldorian analysis. Research Paper No.: 2006/049. Helsinki: UNU-WIDER.

De Oliveira, G., Lima, G.T., 2015. A green Lewis development model. Department of Economics FEA-USP, Working Paper No.: 2015–49.

Duménil, G., Lévy, D., 2001. Costs and benefits of neoliberalism. A class analysis. Rev. Int. Political Econ. 8 (4), 578–607.

Duménil, G., Lévy, D., 2004. The real and financial components of profitability (USA 1948–2000). Rev. Radic. Polit. Econ. 36, 82–110.

Ehrhardt-Martinez, K., Crenshaw, E.M., Jenkins, J.C., 2002. Deforestation and the environmental Kuznets curve: a cross-national investigation of intervening mechanisms. Soc. Sci. Q. 83 (1), 226–243.

Ehrlich, P., Holden, J., 1971. Impact of population growth. Science 171, 1212–1217.

Epstein, G. (Ed.), 2005. Financialization and the World Economy. Edward Elgar Press, Cornwall.

Eskeland, G.A., Harrison, A.E., 2002. Moving to greener pastures? Multinationals and the pollution haven hypothesis. NBER Working Papers 8888, National Bureau of Economic Research, Inc.

Frankel, J.A., Rose, A.K., 2005. Is trade good or bad for the environment? Sorting out the causality. Rev. Econ. Stat. 87 (1), 85–91.

Fuchs V.R. 1968. The Service Economy, National Bureau of Economic Research. New York, United States.

Gollin, D., 2014. The Lewis model: a 60-year retrospective. J. Econ. Perspect. 28 (3), 71–88.

Grossman, G.M., Krueger, A.B., 1991. Environmental impacts of North American free trade agreement. NBER Working Paper Series No.: 3914.

Grossman, G.M., Krueger, A.B., 1995. Economic growth and the environment. Q. J. Econ. 110 (2), 353–377.

Hahnel, R., 2010. Green Economics: Confronting the Ecological Crisis. M.E. Sharpe, New York.

Hamilton, K., Clemens, M., 1999. Genuine savings rates in developing countries. World Bank Econ. Rev. 13 (2), 333–356.

Harris, C.D., 1954. The market as a factor in the localization of industry in the United States. Ann. Assoc. Am. Geogr. 44 (4), 315–348.

Harris, J.R., Todaro, M.P., 1970. Migration, unemployment and development: a two-sector analysis. Am. Econ. Rev. 60 (1), 126–142.

Harvey, D., 1989. The Condition of Postmodernity: An Inquiry Into the Origins of Cultural Change. Blackwell, Cambridge.

Henderson, V., 2010. Cities and development. J. Reg. Sci. 50 (1), 515–540.

Higgins, B., 1956. The "dualistic theory" of underdeveloped areas. Econ. Dev. Cult. Change 4, 499–515.

Hirschman, A.O., 1958. The Strategy of Economic Development. Yale University Press, New Haven, United States.

IEA. 2008. World Energy Outlook 2008. Paris: International Energy Agency.

IEA. 2009. Energy Policies of IEA countries. Paris: International Energy Agency.

IEA. 2012. World Energy Database. Paris: International Energy Agency.

IEA. 2013. Tracking Clean Energy Progress 2013: IEA Input to the Clean Energy Ministerial. Paris, France: OECD/IEA. Available from: http://www.iea.org/publications/TCEP_web.pdf.

IEA. 2016. World Energy Outlook, 2016: Fossil Fuel Subsidy Database. Available from: http://www.worldenergyoutlook.org/resources/energysubsidies/fossilfuelsubsidydatabase/.

Intergovernmental Panel on Climate Change (IPCC), 2013. Climate Change 2013: The Physical Science Basis. Working Group I Contribution to the IPCC Fifth Assessment Report - Changes to the Underlying Scientific/Technical Assessment, (IPCCXXVI/Doc.4), September 27.

IPCC, 2014. Climate Change 2014: Synthesis Report. In: Pachauri, R.K., Meyer, L.A. (Eds.), Contribution of Working Groups I, II and III to the Fifth Assessment Report of the Intergovernmental Panel on Climate Change. IPCC, Geneva, Switzerland.

IUCN, 1980. World Conservation Strategy: Living Resource Conservation for Sustainable Development. Available from: http://data.iucn.org/dbtw-wpd/edocs/WCS-004.pdf.

Jorgenson, D.W., 1961. The development of a dual economy. Econ. J. 71, 309–334.

Jorgenson, D.W., 1966. Testing alternative theories of the development of a dual economy. In: Adelman, I., Thorbecke, E. (Eds.), The Theory and Design of Economic Development. Johns Hopkins, Baltimore.

Jorgenson, D.W., 1967. Surplus agricultural labor and the development of a dual economy. Oxf. Econ. Papers 19 (3), 288–312.

Kaika, D., Zervas, E., 2013. The environmental Kuznets curve (EKC) theory: part A: concept, causes and the CO_2 emissions case. Energy Policy 62, 1392–1402.

Kaldor, N., 1966. Causes of the Slow Rate of Growth in the United Kingdom. Cambridge University Press, Cambridge, UK.

Kaldor, N., 1967. Strategic Factors in Economic Development. Cornell University Press, Ithaca, United States.

Kaufmann, Y.J., et al., 1998. Smoke, clouds, and radiation: Brazil (Scar-B) experiment. J. Geophys. Res. 103, 783–808.

Koplow, D., 1998. Quantifying impediments to fossil fuel trade: an overview of major producing and consuming nations. Prepared for the OECD Trade Directorate.

Kovacevic, A., 2011. Fossil fuel subsidies in the Western Balkans: a report for UNDP. Issued by the Regional Bureau for Europe and the Commonwealth of Independent States (RBEC) in December 2011.

Krippner, G.R., 2005. The financialization of the American economy. Socio-Econ. Rev. 3, 173–208.

Krugman, P., 1991. Increasing returns and economic geography. J. Polit. Econ. 99 (3), 483–499.

Kuznets, S., 1973. Modern economic growth: findings and reflections. Am. Econ. Rev. 63 (3), 247–258.

Lau, L.S., Choong, C.K., Eng, Y.K., 2014. Investigation of the environmental Kuznets curve for carbon emissions in Malaysia: do foreign direct investment and trade matter? Energy Policy 68, 490–497.

Lawrence, P., 2005. Explaining sub-Saharan Africa's manufacturing performance. Dev. Change 36 (6), 1121–1141.

Lewis, W.A., 1954. Economic development with unlimited supplies of labour. Manchester Sch. 22 (2), 139–191.

Lipietz, A., 2012. Korkular ve umutlar: liberal uretkenlik modelinin krizi ve yeşil alternatif. In: Ümit Şahin ve Ahmet Atıl Aşıcı (Ed.), Yeşil Ekonomi. Yeni İnsan Yayınevi, Istanbul.

Lombardo, V., 2012. Modern foundations of dual economy models. CRISEI, Università degli Studi di Napoli. Parthenope Discussion Paper, No. 08.

Masson, P.R., 2001. Migration, human capital, and poverty in a dual-economy of a developing country. IMF Working Paper No. 01/128.

Matsuyama, K., 1992. Agricultural productivity, comparative advantage, and economic growth. J. Econ. Theory 58, 317–334.

McMillan, M., Rodrik, D., Verduzco-Gallo, Í., 2014. Globalization, structural change, and productivity growth, with an update on Africa. World Dev. 63, 11–32.

Meadows, D.H., Meadows, D.L., Randers, J., Behrens, W.W., 1972. The Limits to Growth. Earth Island Limited, London, UK.

Mundlak, Y., 2000. Agriculture and Economic Growth. Harvard University Press, Cambridge, MA.

Murphy, K.M., Shleifer, A., Vishny, R.V., 1989. Industrialization and the big push. J. Political Econ. 97 (5), 1003–1026.

Myrdal, G., 1957. Economic Theory and Underdeveloped Regions. Methuen, London.

Ocampo, J.A., 2008. Structural change and economic growth. In: Ocampo, J.A., Vos, R. (Eds.), Uneven Economic Development. ZED Books, London.

OECD, 2014. Shifting gear: policy challenges for the next 50 years. OECD Economics Department Policy Notes, No. July 24, 2014.

OECD, 2017. Policies for scaling up low-emission and resilient investment. In: Investing in Climate, Investing in Growth, OECD Publishing, Paris. Available from: http://www.oecd.org/environment/investing-in-climate-investing-in-growth 9789264273528-en.htm.

Orhangazi, Ö., 2008. Financialization and the US Economy. Edward-Elgar Publications.

Palma, J.G., 2005. Four sources of deindustrialization and a new concept of the Dutch disease. In: Ocampo, J.A. (Ed.), Beyond Reforms: Structural Dynamics and Macroeconomic Vulnerability (Latin American Development Forum). ECLAC, Washington DC, United States.

Palma, J.G., 2008. De-industrialization, 'premature' deindustrialization and the Dutch disease. In: Durlauf, S.N., Blume, E. (Eds.), The New Palgrave Dictionary of Economics Second Edition. Palgrave.

Poelhekke, S., van der Ploeg, R., 2012. Green havens and pollution havens. DNB Working Paper No. 353.

Rangazas, P., 2013. Introduction: the dual economy approach to economic growth and development. Eurasian Econ. Rev. 3 (1), 1–7.

Rangazas, P., Mourmouras, M., 2013. Wage and fertility gaps in dual economies. Eurasian Econ. Rev. 3 (1), 59–83.

Ranis, G., Fei, J.D.H., 1961. A theory of economic development. Am. Econ. Rev. Vol. 51, 533–565.

Rauch, J.E., 1993. Economic development, urban underemployment, and income inequality. Can. J. Econ. 26 (4), 901–918.

Rees, W., 1992. Ecological footprints and appropriated carrying capacity: what urban economies leaves out. Environ. Urban. 4, 121–130.

Reinert, E.S., 2008. How Rich Countries Got Rich and Why Poor Countries Stay Poor. Public Affairs, London.

Rodrik, D., 2013. Unconditional convergence in manufacturing. Q.J. Econ. 128 (1), 165–204.

Rodrik, D., 2015. Premature deindustrialization. NBER Working Paper No. 20935.

Ros, J., 2000. Development Theory and the Economics of Growth. University of Michigan, Ann Arbor, United States.

Rowthorn, R.E., Ramaswamy, R., 1997. Deindustrialization: Causes and Implications. International Monetary Fund, Washington, United States.

Rowthorn, R.E., Ramaswamy, R., 1999. Growth, trade, and deindustrialization. Staff Pap. Int. Monet. Fund 46, No. 1.

Ruttan, V.W., 1968. Growth stage theories, dual economy models and agricultural development policy. Department of Agricultural Economics University of Minnesota, Publication No. AE 1968/2.

Schumpeter, J.A., 1939. Business cycles: A Theoretical Historical and Statistical Analysis of the Capitalist Process. McGraw–Hill, New York, United States.

Shafik, N., Bandyopadhyay, S., 1992. Economic growth and environmental quality time-series and cross-country evidence. Background Paper for the World Development Report 1992. The World Bank, Washington DC.

Singh, A., 1977. UK industry and the world economy: a case of de-industrialization? Camb. J. Econ. 1 (2), 113–136.

Singh, R.K., Murty, H.R., Gupta, S.K., Dikshit, A.K., 2012. An overview of sustainability assessment methodologies. Ecol. Indic. 15, 281–299.

Stern, D.I., Common, M.S., 2001. Is there an environmental Kuznets curve for sulfur? J. Environ. Econ. Manage. 41, 162–178.

Temple, J.R.W., 2005a. Dual economy models: a primer for growth economists. Manchester Sch. 73 (4), 435–478.

Temple, J.R.W., 2005b. Growth and wage inequality in a dual economy. Bull. Econ. Res. 57 (2), 145–169.

Tregenna, F., 2009. Characterising deindustrialisation: an analysis of changes in manufacturing employment and output internationally. Camb. J. Econ. 33 (3), 433–466.

UNCTAD, 2003. Trade and Development Report: Capital Accumulation Growth and Structural Change. United Nations Publications, New York and Geneva.

UNCTAD, 2016. Trade and Development Report: Structural Transformation for Inclusive and Sustained Growth. United Nations, New York and Geneva.

UNDP, 2000. World Energy Assessment. Available from: http://www.undp.org/content/dam/ aplaws/publication/en/publications/environmentenerg/ www-ee-library/sustainable-energy/world-energy-assessment-energy-and-thechallenge- of-sustainability/World%20 Energy%20Assessment-2000.pdf.

UNEP, 2009. Global Green New Deal. United Nations, Washington DC.

Vollrath, D., 2009a. How important are dual economy effects for aggregate productivity? J. Dev. Econ. 88, 325–334.

Vollrath, D., 2009b. The dual economy in long-run development. J. Econ. Growth 14 (4), 287–312.

Wang, Y., Kang, L., Wu, X., Xiao, Y., 2013. Estimating the environmental Kuznets curve for ecological footprint at the global level: a spatial econometric approach. Ecol. Indic. 34, 15–21.

Wiedman, T., 2009. A review of recent multi-region input–output models used for consumption-based emission and resource accounting. Ecol. Econ. 69 (2), 211–222.

WorldWatch Institute, 2015. Dünyanın Durumu 2015, Türkiye İş Bankası Kültür Yayınları, Türkiye.

World Commission on Environment and Development (WCED), 1987. Our Common Future. Oxford University Press, Oxford.

World Wildlife Fund Nature (WWF), 2012. Türkiye'nin Ekolojik Ayak İzi Raporu, WWF Türkiye, Istanbul.

WRI/CAIT Climate Data Explorer: Historic Greenhouse Gas Emissions. Available from: http://cait.wri.org/historical/Country%20GHG%20Emissions?indicator=Total%20 GH G%20Emissions%20Excluding%20Land.

Young, A.A., 1928. Increasing returns and economic progress. Econ. J. 38 (152), 527–542.

Yuki, K., 2007. Urbanization, informal sector, and development. J. Dev. Econ. 84, 76–103.

FURTHER READING

De Vries, G., 2010. Small retailers in Brazil: are formal firms really more productive? J. Dev. Stud. 46 (8), 1345–1366.

Duménil, G., Lévy, D., 2005. The Costs and Benefits of Neoliberalism: A Class Analysis. In: Epstein, G. (Ed.), Financialization and the World Economy. Edward Elgar Press, Cornwall.

Kuznets, S., 1966. Modern Economic Growth: Rate, Structure, and Speed. Yale University Press, New Haven, United States.

McKinnon, R., 1973. Money and Capital in Economic Development. Brookings Institution, Washington DC, United States.

CHAPTER 3

Energy and Environmental Policy Against Climate Change in Turkey

3.1 STATISTICS ON ENERGY AND ENVIRONMENT IN TURKEY

Economic growth in Turkey has generally not been decoupled from resource use, energy depletion, and environmental degradation. A United Nations report (UN, 2013, p. 3) highlighted that "the present dominant model of development is facing simultaneous multiple crises such as depletion of natural resources and the market failures that have already marked the first decades of the current millennium." Therefore this model of economic growth has been ineffective at enabling productive and decent employment, and has exacerbated the phenomenon of climate change, with its various facets including the depletion of natural resources, the loss of biodiversity, an energy crisis, and food security. In contrast, the report underlined that the "green economy concept proposes to break away from the not very effective current model of development and move towards a more sustainable development paradigm that is merely characterized by low-carbon emissions, rational use of resources and social inclusiveness." These observations are central to green growth, a relatively new concept that has captured the attention of global policy makers, researchers, and civil society organizations, which could help design and evaluate policies that can efficiently achieve environmental sustainability. This is of particular interest to fast-growing emerging market economies, which are characterized by rapidly increasing ecological footprints, and which seek to decouple economic growth from rising energy use and pollution. The lack of such decoupling is observable in Turkey.

3.1.1 Energy Stats

As a developing middle-income country, Turkey has increased its use of electricity and primary energy sources. Turkey's GDP, total energy consumption (oil equivalent), and greenhouse gas (GHG) emissions increased by 1.5-, 1.36-, and 1.13-fold, respectively, from 1990 to 2014. The speed of emission growth has increased since the beginning of the 2000s; however,

Macroeconomics of Climate Change in a Dualistic Economy
http://dx.doi.org/10.1016/B978-0-12-813519-8.00003-0

energy consumption and GHG emissions per GDP decreased slightly. Estimates from the Ministry of Energy and Natural Resources (MENR) indicate that per capita energy use rose from 1241 kg of oil equivalent in 2005 to 1648 kg of oil equivalent in 2015. The total energy demand currently (2015–16) stands at 135.3 million tonnes of oil equivalent.

These statistics hint at a significant projected expansion of energy demand over the next decade. The Turkish Electricity Transmission Company (TEIAS, 2013) estimated that energy demand will continue to increase by 6%–7% annually until 2023; however, this projection is criticized among scholars due to the highly optimistic economic growth assumption used. Official figures project substantial pressures for the continual increase in energy demand, with installed capacity expected to grow from 64 to 120 GW between 2014 and 2023. The underlying implication of such an expectation is that the Turkish economy has not attained stability with respect to its energy demand per capita. Hence supporting the expected level of growth is in itself a challenge that will require significant investments in generation capacity and energy infrastructure, as well as continuation of the energy market reforms initiated in the 2000s.[1] The country's total energy use is still relatively low [approximately one-third of the organization for economic cooperation and development (OECD) average], although it is increasing at a fast pace. The International Energy Agency (IEA, 2013b) predicts that energy use in Turkey will double over the next decade, while electricity demand growth is expected to increase at an even faster pace. Natural gas demand is also expected to increase with the MENR predicting a compound annual growth rate of 2.9% until 2020.

If the forecasted levels of energy demand and energy use are to be attained, Turkey will need to significantly invest in its energy infrastructure. In addition, further investments in the renewable energy sector will also be required to harness the potential of solar and wind power. Conversely, 0.9% of the world total primary energy supply (TPES) is produced in Turkey, which corresponds to a share of 2.3% of OECD's TPES. However, Turkey's TPES/USD 1000 GDP is below other OECD countries

---

[1] In 2001 Turkey commenced a broad electricity reform program with the enactment of the Electricity Market Law (Law No. 4628). This law established a "new and radically different" legal framework for the design of electricity markets, and constituted an independent Energy Market Regulatory Authority (EMRA). Further changes in the electricity market brought about the fragmentation of state-owned enterprises into different entities (i.e., generation, transmission, distribution, wholesale, and retail supply), as well as the introduction of a competitive wholesale electricity market in 2006.

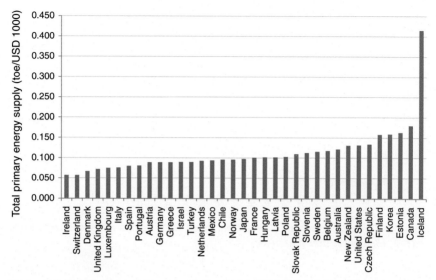

Figure 3.1 *Total primary energy supply (toe/1000 USD) in the OECD, 2015. Toe, Tonnes of oil equivalent. (Data taken from OECD, 2017. Primary Energy Supply (indicator). doi:10.1787/1b33c15a-en).*

such as Mexico, Hungary, Latvia, Poland, and South Korea (Fig. 3.1). The bulk of the country's TPES (around 90%) still originates from fossil fuels and the rest comes from renewable energy sources; natural gas and coal are the main sources of primary energy.

Turkey's energy composition in the mid-2000s saw a decreased contribution from solid fuels and petroleum and an increased contribution from natural gas and renewable energy sources. The contribution of natural gas rose from 5.3 to 32.5% between 1990 and 2014, and the contribution of renewable energy rose from 0.8 to 4.5%. The use of petroleum declined from 45.4 to 26.2% in this same time period. Natural gas produces fewer emissions per unit in comparison to solid fuels; however, as a fossil fuel it is not environmentally friendly. During 1971–90 there was a slight increase in the share of renewable energy in Turkey, but fossil fuel use also increased by 70%. However, renewable energy supplies increased by 20% in the first decade of 2000 (Fig. 3.2). Fossil fuels are still the main source of energy despite the recent acceleration in renewable energy.

Turkey has huge potential to exploit renewable energy sources; however, with the exception of small hydropower plants (SHPPs) and wind power plants, this remains relatively untapped. Turkey ranks seventh in the world and first in Europe in terms of geothermal energy potential

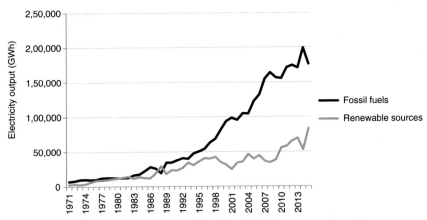

Figure 3.2 *Electricity output (GWh) from fossil fuels versus renewable resources, 1971–2015. (Derived from IEA (2016)).*

(Herdem Attorneys at Law, 2013), with a technical potential of 1500 MW (Baris and Kucukali, 2012). In terms of solar energy, the country has a potential of approximately 3,871,472 MW, while biomass and SHPPs have potentials of 15,995 and 6849 MW, respectively (Benli, 2013). Turkey was listed alongside China, the United States, Germany, and Brazil in a list of the top five countries with solar heat capacity (Ren21, 2013), and was ranked second for annual investments, additions, and production of hydropower capacity and solar water collection (heating) capacity in 2012.[2] Furthermore, Turkey also has one of the highest potentials (114,173 MW) for wind energy in Europe (Baris and Kucukali, 2012). According to the IEA (2013a), wind power projects are successfully competing with subsidies against fossil fuel-based power projects in wholesale electricity markets.

Significant barriers impede the increased use of renewable energy in Turkey. The three general barriers that delay the increased utilization of renewable energy in Europe, Central Asia (Schreiber, 2004, p. 197), and Turkey are:

- the lack of expertise and know-how about renewable energy among energy sector decision makers at government, industry, and local consulting services levels;
- energy market issues including distorted energy policies (e.g., high subsidies for fossil fuels, energy tariffs not covering costs, lack of synchronization between various environmental support programs, and

[2] Based on absolute amounts of investment, power generation capacity, or biofuel production.

the frequent crowding out of potential support by excessive national subsidies) and inadequate and nontransparent legal, regulatory, and institutional frameworks, which leads to uncertainties in the heat and power industry, and to a bias in favor of fossil fuels; and

- high transaction costs due to the typically small size of renewable energy projects compared to large fossil fuel-based projects.

The energy demand across sectors is variable. According to Turkish Statistical Institute (TURKSTAT), the share of electricity production and distribution in sectoral energy demand increased to 42.4% in 2014. The energy demand of the transport and storage sectors reached 9.5% in the same year, while the energy consumption share for the manufacturing industry was 38.4%.

As a result of the increased energy use in energy-intensive sectors, energy imports have risen tremendously and have become an important element of the current account deficit. Turkey has no major oil or gas reserves, therefore it is highly dependent on energy imports (which account for approximately 80% of the total supply) and is highly exposed to the challenge of energy insecurity (Yuksel, 2013). In 2012 Turkey imported 3,980,270 TJ of energy, accounting for around 80% of the total energy supplied that year. The country mostly produces hard coal and lignite; however, domestic consumption is covered by a limited amount of domestic coal production as the extracted reserves are of low quality. Import figures are the highest for oil, followed by natural gas and coal. In 2012 one import of natural gas corresponded to 98% of total domestic demand. Russia and Iran were the main suppliers of oil and natural gas for the same year (IEA, 2013b).

3.1.2 Emissions Stats

In 2015 Turkey's per capita emissions of carbon dioxide (CO_2) and other GHGs (CO_2 eq.) stood at around 6 tons, while its total CO_2 eq. emissions per GDP (in constant USD) reached 0.524 kg. Therefore Turkey displays relatively lower emission figures in comparison to global and OECD averages. However, Turkey is cited in the top five countries with the fastest growth of aggregate CO_2 eq. emissions, which increased from 214 to 475 million tons between 1990 and 2015 (a cumulative increase of 122%; Table 3.1), and is expected to increase to 675 million tons by 2030 (Acar and Yeldan, 2016). This suggests that Turkey will be on a divergent trend to many of the emerging market developing economies, as well as the world average, over the coming decades.

Table 3.1 Greenhouse gas emissions by sectors, 1990–2015

Years	Total emissions (CO₂ eq.)	Change compared to 1990 (%)	Energy sector emissions (CO₂ eq.)	Industrial processes and product use emissions (CO₂ eq.)	Agriculture emissions (CO₂ eq.)	Waste emissions (CO₂ eq.)
1990	214.0	—	134.4	23.7	44.8	11.1
1995	246.6	15.2	163.5	27.3	43.4	12.4
2000	296.5	38.6	211.7	27.8	42.5	14.5
2005	337.2	57.6	241.0	35.9	43.3	16.9
2010	406.8	90.1	291.8	51.0	45.8	18.2
2015	475.1	122.0	340.0	60.7	57.4	16.9

Source: Data taken from TURKSTAT, 2017. Greenhouse Gas Emissions Statistics, 1990–2015.

According to TURKSTAT (2017), CO_2 emissions from the energy sector have more than doubled since 1990 and are expected to rise significantly in the medium and long term due to the increasing energy demand. In 2015 the energy sector was the main contributor (71.5%) to total GHG emissions, followed by industrial processes (13%), agriculture (12%), and waste (3.5%).

Among the OECD countries, Turkey ranked second (after Korea) in terms of the growth rate of GHG emissions during 1990–2012. Fig. 3.3 demonstrates that almost half of all OECD economies experienced negative changes in their emissions during the same period.

3.2 EXISTING ENERGY AND ENVIRONMENTAL POLICIES IN TURKEY

Turkish energy policies are currently based on the depletion of all domestic coal reserves by the end of 2023, and will subsequently be driven by a switch to nuclear energy, which will be activated by the end of the 2020s. However, two points are missing in this trajectory: (1) an environmentally sensitive regional development perspective, and (2) strategic concern for climate change abatement or mitigation.

Nevertheless, these are common strategic policies for many developing economies. Many think that developing countries cannot be asked to reduce emissions until developed countries have done so. The problem of climate change originated from industrialized countries releasing vast levels of GHG emissions, and hence developing countries cannot be held

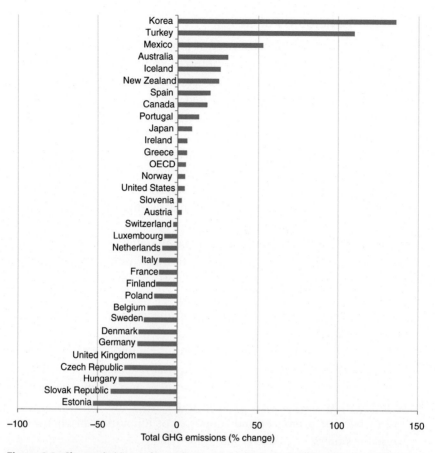

Figure 3.3 *Change (%) in total greenhouse gas emissions of OECD countries, 1990–2012. (Data taken from OECD, 2014. Greenhouse Gas Emissions by Source and the OECD Environment Statistics database. doi:10.1787/data-00594-en. UNFCCC, Greenhouse Gas Inventory Data (2014)).*

responsible. The developing world would like to see industrialized countries committing to reduce emissions before they take any climate action themselves.

We will provide examples of climate policy in the developing world in the upcoming sections; however, this section is mainly devoted to examining tools and policies in relation to energy and climate change in Turkey. Instruments of energy and environmental policy in Turkey have thus far mainly consisted of carbon tax-cum-subsidies and the administration of high taxes on energy market users and suppliers.

3.2.1 Energy-Related Policies

Turkey is grappling with the challenge of providing a cost-competitive energy supply for its population and industrial sector while simultaneously ensuring energy security. Although the country does not have a national energy strategy plan, the MENR created institutional strategic plans to cover the periods 2010–14 and 2015–19. The common objectives of the corresponding plans were:

1. to secure an energy supply by giving priority to domestic resources, by increasing the share of renewable energy resources, by increasing energy efficiency, by making the free market conditions operate fully, by improving the investment environment, and by diversifying resources in the areas of oil and natural gas;
2. to enhance Turkey's influence in regional and global energy by turning the country into an energy hub and terminal using the geostrategic position effectively within the framework of regional cooperation processes;
3. to minimize the negative environmental impacts of energy and natural resource-related activities;
4. to increase the contribution of natural resources into the national economy; to increase the production of industrial raw materials, metals, and nonmetal mineral reserves; and to utilize these on a national scale; and
5. to increase the effectiveness of managing energy and natural resources, and to become a pioneer and supporter of innovation in energy and natural resources.

In addition, Turkey aims to gradually develop nuclear power capacities with a view to reducing its dependency on imported fossil fuels and meeting the growing energy demand. It plans to achieve a nuclear capacity of over 10,000 MW by 2030, and has started cooperating with Russia in the construction and operation of a nuclear power plant. A second nuclear power plant is planned for Sinop and a third project is under discussion.

Fossil Fuel Subsidies: Coal, Oil, and Gas

In order to meet its rising energy demand and decrease its dependence on energy imports, Turkey has supported the coal sector with generous subsidies, which range from direct transfers from the treasury to government support for coal exploration. In 2012 the country introduced an investment incentive scheme, which contained various instruments to support new coal mining and power generation projects depending on the region that the investment was to take place. However, these subsidies have the potential to compromise the environment, disrupt the development of low-carbon technologies, and undermine public finances. Previous work by the Global Subsidies Initiative and their Turkish partners (Acar et al., 2015) established a detailed understanding of the current level of knowledge around the role of subsidies to the coal industry, and they identified particular subsidies for which direct cost estimates were not available. Available rudimentary data revealed that quantifiable subsidies to the coal sector result in a per kWh subsidy of around USD 0.01, which increases to USD 0.02 when consumer subsidies are included. A total of USD 730 million was given to the coal sector in the form of subsidies in 2013 (Acar et al., 2015, p. 10). When including the exploration subsidies for oil and gas, the sum (USD 1283 million) represents approximately 0.16% of Turkey's nominal GDP in 2013.

In order to assess the effects of the existing coal subsidization scheme on emissions, energy security, economic and social costs, income, employment, and economic growth, Acar and Yeldan (2016) conducted an applied general equilibrium analysis. They established that if coal production and investment subsidies were eliminated by 2030, CO_2 emissions would decrease significantly in both high- and low-income regions of Turkey. Such a policy change would bring about a 5.4% decrease in emissions by 2030 compared to the base path. Given that the coal sector comprises only a small portion of the sectoral production of the country, it is clear that eliminating coal subsidies would be significantly beneficial in terms of combating environmental pollution and climate change. Existing coal subsidies compromise the competitiveness of renewable energy technologies and jeopardize renewable energy investments, as well as making the energy system dependent on fossil fuel-based energy (i.e., "lock-in") (Bridle and Kitson, 2014).

Renewable Energy Policy

Turkey enacted its first specific law regarding renewable energy, the Utilization of Renewable Energy Sources for the Purpose of Generating Electrical Energy (the Renewable Energy Law, No. 5346), on May 18, 2005. This was a key step towards strengthening the country's renewable energy sector and meeting the growing energy demand. The law stated that the legal entity holding a generation license shall be granted a "renewable energy resource (RES) certificate" by EMRA for the purpose of monitoring the domestic and international markets of RES-generated electricity. Furthermore, this law provided feed-in tariffs, which were purchase guarantees until 2011.

Table 3.2 Feed-in tariffs for renewable energy in Turkey

Energy types	Tariff (US¢/kWh)	Local production premium (US¢/kWh)	Maximum tariff (US¢/kWh)
Hydro	7.3	2.3	9.6
Wind	7.3	3.7	11.0
Geothermal	10.5	2.7	13.2
Biomass	13.3	5.6	18.9
Solar photovoltaic	13.3	6.7	20.0
Concentrating solar power	13.3	9.2	22.5

Source: Amending Law to the Renewable Energy Law (December 29, 2010) Law No. 6094.

It allowed entities generating renewable energy to rent state territories or provided the right to access (or permission to use) these territories.

An amendment to the Renewable Energy Law was later introduced to improve the incentives and encourage renewable energy investment in Turkey. New favorable tariffs were introduced for the sale of electricity generated by renewable energy sources, as well as further feed-in tariffs[3] that were available for 10 years from commissioning of the plant. Table 3.2 displays the current levels of feed–in tariffs offered to renewable energy producers in Turkey. Solar power and biomass projects receive the highest feed-in tariffs (13.3 US¢/kWh), while hydropower and wind power producers are granted 7.3 US¢/kWh. Those projects that use domestic equipment for electricity production are also rewarded with local production premium support, which is determined by the type of energy source. The maximum amount of support may reach up to 22.5 US¢/kWh for concentrating solar power projects.

In accordance with the strategy plans and Renewable Energy Law, the country is hoping that 30% of power generation will come from renewable sources by 2023. The government aims to achieve 20,000 MW of installed wind capacity, 600 MW of installed solar power capacity, and full utilization of its hydro potential by 2023.

3.2.2 Environmental Policy

Turkey's climate change policies are set out in the National Climate Change Strategy (2010–23) and the National Climate Change Action Plan (2011–23). The former identifies actions against climate-related outcomes

---

[3] Feed-in tariffs are fixed cash per kWh payments that were determined by an administrative body and generally available for eligible energy producers.

and sets carbon intensity reduction targets and emission reduction targets (for CO_2) from the energy sector (i.e., a 7% reduction of 1990 levels by 2020). However, while Turkey is a signatory to the Kyoto Protocol, it remains the only OECD country without a national GHG emissions target, and has not made a commitment to reducing GHG emissions by 2020. The country is still to take a clear and strong position.

The most up-to-date document that sets out Turkey's national emission reduction target is the intended nationally determined contributions (INDC) document, which was submitted to the UNFCCC Secretariat on September 30, 2015, prior to the Conference of the Parties (COP) 21 meeting in Paris. This document summarizes Turkey's national situation and emphasizes its status as a country with special circumstances (a status recognized by decision No. 1/CP.16 of the UNFCCCs Annex 1). The document states that Turkey defines its emission reductions and adaptation strategies within this framework. In this document, which is intended to be implemented in 2012–30, Turkey declares its commitment to reduce the 1175 million tons of CO_2 eq. GHG emissions predicted under the base scenario, to 929 million tons by 2030 (a reduction rate of 21%). It states that, in doing so, an important step will have been taken towards low-carbon development with a view to achieving the 2°C global target.[4]

The INDC declaration also cites plans and policies that will be adapted for emission-intensive sectors. However, the declaration includes no data or projections regarding the emission reductions that these policies and measures are expected to deliver in comparison to those predicted under the business-as-usual (BAU) scenario in the 2021–30 period. Box 3.1 includes the main targets established in these key plans and policies. Emission reductions to be achieved by the abovementioned policies and plans compared to the BAU scenario are presented in Fig. 3.4.

In order to meet the targets set forth by the national contribution document, it may be useful to go through the existing relevant national and sectoral plans and policy frames (i.e., the Tenth Development Plan (2014–18), National Climate Change Strategy (2010–23), Climate Change Action Plan (2011–23), Industrial Strategy Document (2015–18), Energy Efficiency Strategy Document (2012–23), Electric Energy Market and Security of Supply Strategy Document (2009), and strategic plans of other relevant ministries). Even though the targets and

---

[4] Republic of Turkey Intended Nationally Determined Contribution. Available from: https://www.csb.gov.tr/db/iklim/editordosya/The_INDC_of_TURKEY_v_15_19_30-TR.pdf.

BOX 3.1 Key plans and policies for mitigation

Energy
- Increasing electricity production capacity from solar power to 10 GW by 2030.
- Increasing electricity production capacity from wind power to 16 GW by 2030.
- Tapping the full hydroelectric potential.
- Commissioning a nuclear power plant by 2030.
- Reducing electricity transmission and distribution losses to 15% by 2030.
- Rehabilitating public electricity generation power plants.
- Establishing microgeneration and cogeneration systems and producing on-site electricity.

Industry
- Reducing emission intensity with the implementation of the National Strategy and Action Plan on Energy Efficiency.
- Increasing energy efficiency in industrial installations and providing financial support to energy efficiency projects.
- Performing studies to increase the use of waste as an alternative fuel for appropriate sectors.

Transport
- Ensuring a balanced utilization of transport modes in freight and passenger transport by reducing the share of road transport and increasing the share of maritime and rail transport.
- Enhancing combined transport.
- Implementing sustainable transport approaches in urban areas.
- Promoting alternative fuels and clean vehicles.
- Reducing fuel consumption and emissions of road transport with the National Intelligent Transport Systems Strategy Document (2014–23) and its Action Plan (2014–16).
- Realizing high-speed railway projects.
- Increasing urban railway systems.
- Saving fuel using tunnel projects.
- Removing old vehicles from traffic.
- Implementing green port and green airport projects to ensure energy efficiency.
- Implementing special consumption tax exemptions for maritime transport.

Buildings and Urban Transformation
- Constructing new energy-efficient residential and service buildings in accordance with the Energy Performance of Buildings Regulations.

- Creating energy performance certificates for new and existing buildings to control energy consumption and GHG emissions and to reduce energy consumption/m².
- Reducing the consumption of primary energy sources in new and existing buildings through design, technological equipment, and building materials, and developing channels that promote the use of renewable energy sources (e.g., loans and tax reductions).
- Disseminating green building, passive-energy, zero-energy house designs to minimize the energy demand and ensure local production of energy.

Agriculture
- Saving fuel through land consolidation in agricultural areas.
- Rehabilitating grazing lands.
- Controlling the use of fertilizers and implementing modern agricultural practices.
- Supporting minimum tillage methods.

Waste
- Sending solid wastes to managed landfill sites.
- Reusing, recycling, and using other processes to recover secondary raw materials to use as energy source or to remove wastes.
- Recovering energy from waste using processes such as material recycling of wastes, biodrying, biomethanization, composting, advanced thermal processes, or incineration.
- Recovering methane from landfill gas from managed and unmanaged landfill sites.
- Utilizing industrial wastes as alternative raw materials or fuels in other industrial sectors through an industrial symbiosis approach.
- Conducting relevant studies to utilize wastes generated from breeding and poultry farms.
- Rehabilitating unmanaged waste sites and ensuring wastes be deposited at managed landfill sites.

Forestry
- Increasing sink areas and preventing land degradation.
- Implementing the Action Plan on Forestry Rehabilitation and National Afforestation Campaign.

Source: UNFCCC. Intended Nationally Determined Contribution (Turkey).

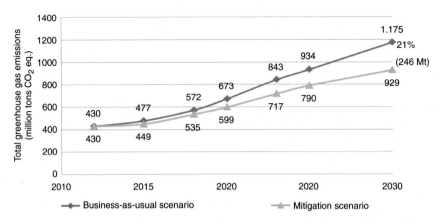

Figure 3.4 *Greenhouse gas emissions in the mitigation versus business-as-usual scenario, according to the INDC of Turkey. (UNFCCC. Intended Nationally Determined Contribution (Turkey)).*

policies set forth in these documents, which form the basis of the INDC, refer to such keywords as environmental awareness, climate change, clean production, and resource efficiency, the contributions of these policies to reducing emissions or protecting the environment are not expressed in quantitative terms. More quantifiable data is needed in order to evaluate the adequacy of the INDC.

3.3 POSSIBLE EXTENSIONS OF ENVIRONMENTAL POLICY IN TURKEY

In environmental economics literature, two main instruments stand out as market-based mechanisms (MBMs) that can be implemented against climate change: (1) quota allocation-based emission trading systems (ETS) and voluntary carbon markets; and (2) taxation (e.g., carbon tax) or subsidies (e.g., energy efficiency subsidies, subsidies for renewable energy technologies, or guaranteed purchases for renewable energy).[5]

The most prominent practice of ETS was designed by EU members within the scope of the Kyoto Protocol. In addition, energy efficiency certificates (white certificates) and renewable energy trading systems also exist, which aim to encourage energy efficiency and the use of renewable energy sources. New practices may be added to these in line with evolving market conditions.

[5] We widely benefited from Yeldan et al. (2016) for the detailed information on alternative instruments in this section.

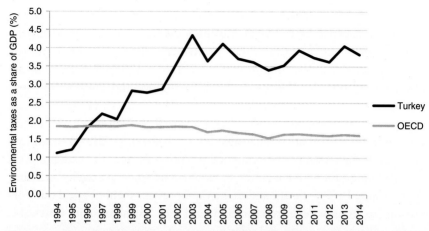

Figure 3.5 *Environmental taxes as a share of GDP, 1994–2014. (OECD (www.oecd.org)).*

Both mechanisms have strengths and weaknesses in terms of their goals. For example, emission control based on carbon trading is more compatible with market rationale; however, one may encounter serious problems during the *monitoring, reporting, and verification* (MRV) stages. In addition, decisions regarding the method for allocating trading quotas, whether positive pricing will be implemented during allocation, and how the price will be determined are of strategic importance to the functioning of the ETS system.

Conversely, control mechanisms based on taxation cause rigidities between direct producers and end users and influence the decisions of market participants. Taxes, renewable energy subsidies, project support for increasing energy efficiency, and regulations on energy efficiency in buildings are among the main instruments that could serve the development of a low-carbon economy in Turkey. However, the relatively high taxes (particularly per unit price of electricity and motor fuel in Turkey), which are also incorporated in the financial regulations on environmental protection, do not serve the purpose of achieving meaningful progress in reducing CO_2 emissions. For instance, Fig. 3.5 demonstrates an environmental tax burden that amounts to 4%–5% of national income in Turkey. It is noteworthy that the definition of environmentally related taxes also encompasses energy and fuel taxes, which are not necessarily levied with any environmental concerns. In comparison, the environmental tax rate in OECD countries is approximately 1%–1.5%. Despite this, the growth of CO_2 emissions cannot be held in check in Turkey, therefore the exclusive use of taxation has failed to successfully protect the environment and mitigate climate change.

The main problem here is that, despite taxation, there has been a failure to develop alternatives to the energy-intensive linear processes with low-resource efficiency. In cases where alternative options are not promoted, the only outcomes from high taxation are mounting production costs and increased revenues for the government. In addition, no meaningful progress is achieved in mitigating the environmental effects. However, across Europe and in other industrialized countries, improving energy efficiency and developing alternative renewable energy sources are the preconditions for successfully tackling environmental pollution. Rather than adopting tax practices that serve to increase the costs of environmental policies and budget revenues, Turkey should undertake the necessary technological transformations to improve energy efficiency and seek to incorporate renewable energy sources (i.e., wind and solar power) into its economy.

3.3.1 Emissions Trading Systems and the Turkish Experience

Despite being an Annex 1 country, Turkey is not included in the Kyoto Protocol's Annex B due to its special circumstances.[6] Therefore no emission limits have been set for Turkey, and it is currently not in a position to benefit from these flexible mechanisms or participate in relevant markets. Therefore Turkey has to date been trading solely in the voluntary carbon market.

The voluntary carbon market is a scheme that, so far, seems to approximate the ETS to the greatest degree. The trading volume of the voluntary carbon market was observed to be USD 4.5 billion between 2004 and 2011, as a result of which 1 billion tons of CO_2 emissions were offset. Turkey accounted for USD 207 million of the voluntary trading during this period, which enabled it to offset 31.7 million tons of emissions. The Ministry of Environment and Urbanization (MEU) reported that Turkey had 308 projects registered in the voluntary carbon market in 2014, amounting to 20 million tons of CO_2 allocation.[7] According to the two mechanisms of voluntary emission reduction standards (the voluntary carbon standard and the gold standard), Turkey is the third largest supplier after China and India. In 2015 Turkey supplied 3.2 million tons of CO_2 eq., but was found to offer

---

[6] Since Turkey is one of the founders of the OECD, which mainly consists of developed and industrialized countries, it is considered among the "developed" countries by the UN-FCCC. However, the UNFCCC states that Turkey has "special circumstances" as it is a developing economy, which is not considered as an emerging economy or a country in transition. For further details see Turhan et al. (2016).

[7] http://www.csb.gov.tr/projeler/iklim/index.php?Sayfa=sayfa&Tur=webmenu&Id=12461.

the lowest price (USD 1.3 per ton) among the 20 supplying countries. Of the offsets Turkey supplied, 97% came from renewable energy sources.

Control mechanisms based on carbon trading systems are regarded as another nascent instrument for Turkey. The most critical aspect of the ETS relates to the MRV of emissions. To ensure the efficient functioning of the system, accredited verification institutions and public agencies and institutions may be required to carry out these transactions. Difficulties experienced during the reporting of emission data may result in the suspension of countries from their trading system. For example, Greece[8] and Bulgaria[9] were previously suspended from carbon trading mechanisms on the grounds that they failed to comply with the United Nations GHG emission reporting rules. Having recently been included in voluntary markets, Turkey must undertake to set up, within the context of its EU membership perspective, the necessary legal infrastructure for operating a MRV system in accordance with the EU ETS. To this end, Turkey issued the "Regulation on Monitoring of Greenhouse Gas Emissions"[10] on June 25, 2012; the "Communiqué on Monitoring and Reporting of Greenhouse Gas Emissions"[11] on July 22, 2014; and the "Communiqué on Verification of Greenhouse Gas Emissions and Accreditation of Verifiers"[12] on April 2, 2015.

Strengths, weaknesses, opportunities, threats (SWOT) analyses, conducted by the MEU, identified the most significant shortcomings and challenges that impede the development of the ETS in Turkey include an insufficient degree of deepening in national financial markets, a lack of institutional competence on the part of financial control mechanisms, and a failure to eliminate deficiencies in control and monitoring systems (MEU, 2016).

Even though Turkey has not been able to make use of the financial resources earmarked for climate change mitigation that have been provided to countries with similar economic indicators, climate change mitigation has become a key agenda item for Turkey. The fact that Turkey could not previously benefit from flexibility mechanisms under the Kyoto Protocol and had to carry out high-cost technology transfers, has undermined the country's efforts to develop the sufficient financial resources required to reduce emissions and accommodate the negative effects of climate change. As a consequence

---

[8] http://www.enn.com/pollution/article/35122.

[9] http://www.reuters.com/article/us-bulgaria-co2-suspension-idUSTRE65S-3RU20100629.

[10] http://www.resmigazete.gov.tr/eskiler/2014/05/20140517-3.htm.

[11] http://www.resmigazete.gov.tr/eskiler/2014/07/20140722-5.htm.

[12] http://www.resmigazete.gov.tr/eskiler/2015/04/20150402-12.htm.

the emergence of established practices in Turkey regarding building capacities, raising awareness, and adopting cost-efficient emissions reduction options within the context of carbon trading system has been delayed.

Conversely, the recent momentum in renewable energy investments, where emission reduction certificates that have been traded in voluntary markets since 2006 are obtained, constitutes an important step towards the emergence of an emission trading market for Turkey. There have been substantial reductions in the EU ETS and regional carbon prices following the 2008 crisis. Nonetheless, the revisions made to the Renewable Energy Law in 2010 have contributed to the continuation of renewable energy investments (Ari and Sari, 2015). At the same time, the Partnership for Market Readiness (PMR) project, coordinated by the MEU, was initiated to achieve institutional capacity building regarding the ETS. It is hoped that this project will mobilize the country's emission trading potential, provided that favorable market conditions emerge in the future and that Turkey takes its place in the global climate regime in line with its "common but differentiated responsibilities and respective capabilities" under the UNFCCC. However, it should be noted that projects with high additionality can benefit from the ETS. As a G20 country with a growing economy, Turkey's reduction portfolio should not rely exclusively on the ETS for emission reduction projects and activities.

3.3.2 Partnership for Market Readiness Project

Endeavors intended to develop MBMs in Turkey are being carried out using funds provided by the World Bank within the framework of the PMR. As it attempts to address alternative market-based instruments for carbon pricing, and assess the suitability of each instrument by analyzing Turkey's existing institutional infrastructure, this project tackles five other instruments in addition to the ETS, including: (1) carbon taxation; (2) energy efficiency trading; (3) renewable energy trading; (4) result-oriented financing; and (5) comprehensive crediting.

Discussions are being held regarding the design and implementation of each alternative instrument, the compatibility of instruments with existing policies and with one another, the legal and institutional gap analysis, and the revenue utilization methods.

Carbon Taxation

The legal and institutional basis required for the carbon taxation mechanism is not yet in place in Turkey. Since sectoral carbon taxes can only be determined using GHG emission data, the availability of the MRV mechanism is a precondition for this system.

Energy Efficiency Trading (Trading of Energy Efficiency Certificates)
A strong legal and institutional infrastructure, which is necessary for the implementation of this mechanism, is not yet available in Turkey. As mentioned above, an MRV system should also be established for energy efficiency.

Renewable Energy Certificates Trading (REC Trading)
There is also no readily available legal basis for REC trading in Turkey. Improving the current laws and regulations concerning renewable energy is imperative for the functioning of such a system.

Result-Oriented Financing
Result-oriented financing is a form of financing offered in exchange for the implementation of a project and the provision of a service. The state (or other funding institutions) provide financial support for programs that make investments in accordance with predetermined emission reduction targets and successfully meet these targets.

Comprehensive Crediting Mechanism
The clean development mechanism, which is a "project based" certificate trading mechanism, forms the basis of a comprehensive crediting mechanism. What distinguishes a comprehensive crediting mechanism is that it is developed within the scope of a national or regional program. Emission reductions achieved by sectoral, national, or regional scale programs, and policy tools providing credits for performances extending beyond a predetermined emission target or threshold, are certified and traded. This is regarded as a MBM suitable for rapidly-growing sectors.

Given Turkey's current preliminary institutional and legal arrangements, comprehensive crediting and result-oriented financing are the most feasible options compared to the other alternatives. Steps towards an MRV mechanism are reported to be underway.

Another significant endeavor under the PMR project has been discussions on Turkey's legal preparations. The gap analysis conducted during these discussions revealed that laws and regulations, particularly in the field of MRV in Turkey, have already been studied, and future endeavors should focus on how this system can be designed in an EU ETS compatible way (MEU, 2016). Determination of ETS quotas and identification of allocation methods are two of the main priority areas. Conversely, the stability and predictability of the carbon market and prices have not yet been adequately ensured at the international level. It is anticipated that international expertise on these issues will needed to be transferred to Turkey.

Even though the direct processes of quota determination and allocation have not yet been initiated in Turkey, the PMR study has established that the 21% reduction target put forward by the INDC may be used as an example. As the INDCs overall target will be reviewed every 5 years, it is considered possible to design quota allocations in the PMR documentation on the basis of the INDC commitment target. The fact that the existing INDC projections do not include sectoral differentiations leads to uncertainties concerning the scheme. On the other hand, as seen within the context of the macroeconomic model below, economic transformations that are consistent with Turkey's 21% (reductions from BAU) target will constitute a significant input to this decision.

In quota allocation, two options stand out in the PMR documentation. The first option relates to the *absolute quota limitation under fixed reserves*. It has the advantage of offering precise and clear goals in the pilot implementation stage. With this option, prospective allocations can be determined on the basis of historical observations in a way that is consistent with the INDCs overall target. Under the current INDC target, these allocations amount to a 1.3% decline in carbon intensity.

The second option in quota allocation can be defined as *growth-oriented absolute quota allocation*. Here, variable or flexible reserves may be allocated to new participants depending on the quota level, the INDC-compatible carbon intensity reduction target (1.3%), and growth projections for the economy (for the relevant sector). Therefore new participants will be integrated into the system and the emergence of "big" players in the system may be avoided.

The main shortcoming of both options is their failure to provide sufficiently detailed carbon emission data at the sectoral level, therefore data inventory improvements are crucial for the implementation of this step. In particular, possible fluctuations in business cycles raises serious concerns regarding the updating of such data inventories, as well as the predictability of the growth path. In this context, it is assessed that a proper ETS may be established after firms have acquired MRV experience. Nevertheless, it is important that a dynamic, rather than a fixed growth-oriented, approach be adopted when determining the upper limit in the system, and that firms be consulted for assessing their long-term plans and sectoral growth projections, as well as the sector's own dynamics.

Some of the most significant experience that Turkey can attain regarding the EU ETS relates to the issue of *carbon price volatility and predictability*. Carbon price, as a "market price," should undoubtedly be allowed to float freely; however, in this type of market market, drastic reductions in the price can slow the emission trading activities, while very high prices tend to increase trading risks as well as the system's burden on production costs. The PMR documentation defines three alternative systems based on the European experience:

- *Price corridor:* In this system, upper and lower price limits are determined using historical data and business cycle projections. Its technical convenience is among its major advantages; however, the necessity to actively maintain the width of the corridor may lead to fairness and reliability issues in practice.
- *Market price reserve system:* This system will be implemented by the EU in 2019. Minimization of interventions to market rationale is the main advantage of this system; however, the main drawback for Turkey is its potential to cause uncertainties in the pilot implementation period.
- *Supply-side measures:* Alongside the price corridor, "bidding" is intended to be actively used in this system. Active supply-side policy measures will reinforce the will of the system's regulating authority although it may also add to the uncertainties in the system.

The ETS pilot scheme seeks to transfer MRV expertise to market decision makers and is intended for use for a maximum of 3 years. The ETS pilot scheme is envisaged to rest on the elements cited below (for further information see the PMR documentation of the MEU):

- *Scope:* The ETS pilot scheme can be structured to conform with the MRV design.
- *Quota level and allocation:* The total quota level can be specified in accordance with sectoral production levels or growth predictions. Here, a 1.3% annual decline in carbon intensity may be targeted based on the average of the last 3 years of historical emission data and with the INDC target. A common denominator for reductions may also be added to the design in order to ensure harmonization among sectors.
- *Offset design:* Offsets may be utilized for emission reduction projects that were put into effect up until 4 years before the commencement date of the pilot scheme, provided that these projects are included in the gold standard or voluntary carbon standard system.
- *Provisional flexibility:* Banking and borrowing options may be offered during the pilot implementation stage.

- *Market entry and trading*: Emission trading accounts should be centrally filed. They may be open to the firms within the ETS and to domestic financial institutions. Financial system rules will be confined exclusively to the trading of permits and will preclude other permit-derived instruments.
- *Sanctions*: Sanctions will only be imposed to ensure the observance of compliance rules and will be gradually lifted during the pilot implementation period.
- *Linkages:* The pilot ETS will not be linked to any other ETS.

It is well-documented that price instruments administered through the market alone are not sufficient to achieve the broad objectives of controlling global GHG concentrations, or to fully assist in maintaining a sustainable and eco-friendly growth path (Acar et al., 2014). Part of the problem is that the development of novel eco-friendly technologies typically involves positive spillovers in the form of agglomeration effects, knowledge diffusion, cross-firm externalities, and industry-wide learning; however, the decentralized optimization embedded in the laissez-faire actions of the markets may fail to capture these positive spillovers. Market failures are at the root of these problems, as although basic (economic and regulatory) instruments are available, their systematic use in broader policy packages has been lacking. In addition, there is a need to reevaluate the concept of green growth from a regional perspective if one intends to focus on the spatial implications of sustained growth.

3.4 POST-PARIS AGENDA AND AN INTERNATIONAL COMPARISON OF DEVELOPING COUNTRIES WITH RESPECT TO CLIMATE CHANGE POLICIES

The Paris Agreement was adapted at the COP 21 summit held in Paris in December 2015, ratified by a sufficient number of countries throughout 2016, and entered into force on November 4, 2016. This agreement marks the beginning of a new era in the international climate regime. The fact that the agreement entered into force within less than a year after its adoption undoubtedly represents profound progress with regards to global climate change cooperation. Nevertheless, a busy negotiation agenda awaits the global climate diplomacy between 2016 and 2020.

Being an Annex 1 country within the UNFCCC means that Turkey assumes the same responsibilities as developed countries.[13] Consequently, Turkey had to ensure that its special status was recognized during negotiations

---

[13] We made use of Yeldan et al. (2016) to summarize the stance of Turkey with respect to global climate change diplomacy in this section.

on implementing the rules of the convention and the Kyoto Protocol. After prolonged deliberations, Turkey's special status within the UNFCCC was recognized, but its status under the Paris Agreement remains unclear. This situation causes ambiguities as to how Turkey will benefit from financial resources, capacity building, and technology transfer supports earmarked for developing countries. Although the French and Moroccan presidencies made a joint statement to assure that "no party should be disadvantaged or excluded from the collective development of the rulebook simply because it is still in the process of joining the agreement," the process may take a different turn (UNFCCC, 2016). Prolonging Turkey's accession process due to the ambiguity concerning its status should not inhibit the country's effective contribution to negotiations on the implementation of the Paris Agreement, and Turkey should reinforce its efforts to that effect.

The Paris Agreement reflects a global consensus to limit the average temperature rise to well below 2°C, even to 1.5°C if possible; however, national contributions submitted to the UNFCCC Secretariat suggested that global temperatures will be 2.7–3.7°C warmer by the end of the century. The discrepancy between national contributions and the 1.5–2°C target is called the "emission gap." To eliminate this gap it is imperative to reinforce the targets pertaining to the periods before and after 2020. In accordance with the agreement, the launching of a global dialogue on the revision of national contributions is envisaged to occur in 2018, as reduction targets are to be evaluated and strengthened every 5 years.

Turkey has pledged a 21% economy-wide emission cut under BAU by 2030, a goal that would allow its emissions to more than double over the next 15 years, increasing emissions by 116% in 2030 compared with 2012 levels. Such a plan would see Turkey's emissions increase at an even faster rate than its growth over the past 10 years.

It is essential to assess Turkey's INDC document in light of both the consensus embodied in the Paris Agreement and of other practices and strategic documents related to priority sectors. As mentioned above, the reduction scenario in Turkey's national contribution document foresees that its emissions will be reduced to 929 million tons of CO_2 eq. by 2030; in other words, the emissions will be double the 2013 level.[4] This means that its emission growth rate will be 40% higher in 2010–30 than in 1990–2010. From this perspective it is evident that Turkey should earnestly focus on the 5-year revisions stipulated by the Paris Agreement. Turkey's INDC has been rated as "inadequate" by Climate Action Tracker.

Conversely, Mexico has set a more ambitious emission reduction target, and aims to be 22% below baseline in 2030, which corresponds to an emission increase of 56% above its 1990 levels. Similarly Brazil, one of the ten largest emitters, aims to limit GHG emissions [including land use, land-use change and forestry (LULUCF)] to 1.3 and 1.2 $GtCO_2$ eq. by 2020 and 2030, respectively. Such targets are equivalent to a 37% and 43% reduction below 2005 levels, respectively. South Africa, despite being rated "inadequate," aims to reduce its emissions to 398–614 $MtCO_2$ eq. (including LULUCF) during 2025–2030, stabilize its emissions over 2025–35, and finally reduce total emissions over the longer term. Ethiopia aims to decrease its emissions by 64% below the BAU scenario by 2030. The INDCs of Mexico and Brazil are rated as "medium," whereas Ethiopia's is rated as "sufficient" by Climate Action Tracker (2016).[14]

3.5 CONCLUSION AND DISCUSSION: AVAILABLE OPTIONS TO TACKLE WITH CLIMATE CHANGE

Scientific findings demonstrate that the new systems established by mankind in the post-Industrial Revolution era have radically changed the global climate to an unprecedented degree. Levels of GHGs in the atmosphere (i.e., carbon and methane) have considerably increased in the last 200 years, reaching a level not seen in 800,000 years. The global atmospheric CO_2 intensity, which had an average of 280 ppm prior to industrialization and never exceeded 300 ppm, went beyond 350 ppm in the 1980s, and is beyond 400 ppm as of today.

The United Nations Intergovernmental Panel on Climate Change issued its fourth assessment report (AR4) in 2007. This report focused on keeping the global CO_2 intensity below 450 ppm and limiting the global temperature rise to below 2°C, with a view of ultimately preventing the climate balance from being irreversibly disrupted. However, since the year the report was published, the carbon concentration has risen by 20 units in less than a decade.

The same report purports that the increased frequency of incidents (i.e., the ever-changing extreme weather conditions, droughts, decline in agricultural production, floods, sea level rise, new risks to human health, and ecosystem degradation) are also linked to the radical change we inflicted on the climate. The report emphasizes that the failure to limit temperature rise and launch adaptive mechanisms will intensify the abovementioned conditions in an unpredictable manner.

---

[14] http://climateactiontracker.org/indcs.html.

The Paris Agreement entered into force on November 4, 2016, following its adoption at the COP 21 summit in Paris in December 2015, and its ratification throughout the year by a sufficient number of countries. This agreement heralds the beginning of a new era in the international climate regime, and in this era it will not be viable to pursue a national policy relying on the premises of the Kyoto Protocol. The most prominent feature of this new era is that it requires all state parties, both developed and developing, to take measures to reduce emissions in accordance with the agreement's precept of "common but differentiated responsibilities and respective capabilities." This marks the end of the period under the Kyoto Protocol where only developed countries attempted to reduce emissions pursuant to concrete and quantitative targets. Developing countries only participated in the process on a voluntary basis through sectoral action plans and without setting any reduction targets. In the post-Paris Agreement period, both developed and developing countries are expected to take part in the global fight against climate change by determining their reduction targets themselves depending on their historical responsibilities and national capacities.

Turkey will be increasingly compelled to go along with the global tendency to reduce carbon intensity. In this new era, Turkey will need to transform all major carbon-generating sectors, increase the share of renewables in the primary energy mix, swiftly improve energy efficiency, adapt high-emission industrial sectors, and develop low-carbon transportation methods (i.e., railways and combined transportation).

Turkey's untapped renewable energy potential can be considered as an opportunity from economic and environmental perspectives. The country has progressed in several areas of energy policy since 2005, and there are signs of better balance in energy policy goals in the future. To promote the development of renewable energy and to utilize Turkey's renewable energy potential, Fossil Fuel Subsidies (FFS) can be reallocated to renewable energy projects to increase the level of support provided. The basic economics of renewable energy need to be altered by increasing the cost of fossil fuel-based energy (e.g., through taxes or equivalent mechanisms), by reducing the costs of renewable energy (e.g., subsidies), or by boosting the returns to renewable energies (e.g., through paying a premium for this form of energy).

Energy efficiency, in particular, will assume a prominent role in emission reductions, as evidenced by global trends and in the IEAs analyses. It will also be crucial to transition to a system where renewable energy sources have a larger share and are more widely used, as is seen at the global level.

Renewables have accounted for two-thirds of the capacity increase in Turkey's electricity sector in the last 3 years, and this momentum is expected to accelerate. Nonetheless, subsidies and legal arrangements for fostering alternative sectors must be handled *in conjunction with market instruments*. Improving Turkey's measuring, monitoring, and reporting capacities; improving its transparency regarding its emissions and relevant policies; and regulating its accountability are also indispensable for the smooth implementation and functioning of emission reduction policies. In addition to emission reduction, the benefits of transitioning to a low-carbon economy such as the prevention of air pollution, the reduction of energy import dependency, and the creation of new employment opportunities, should also be evaluated within this context.

Turkey's need for an inclusive multifactor climate policy-making process still prevails. The insurance and financial sectors, which are directly exposed to the present and future ramifications of climate change, should take an appropriate position and be prepared in this regard. Climate policies not only signify a multilayered issue influencing a multitude of sectors, but also necessitate extensive knowledge, scientific research, and discussion with respect to possible solutions and emerging global trends. For this reason it is important to ensure that in the process of devising policies for climate change mitigation, multilateral negotiations continue to involve the public sector, businesses, academies, and nongovernmental organizations.

MBMs that can be implemented against climate change are grouped into two general approaches in the environmental economics literature: (1) taxation or subsidies, and (2) quota allocation-based carbon trading systems. The most prominent example among carbon trading systems was designed by EU members within the scope of the Kyoto Protocol. Both approaches have strengths and weaknesses in terms of their goals. Emission control based on carbon trading is more compatible with market rationale; however, one may encounter serious problems during the supervision and monitoring stages. In addition, decisions regarding which method will be adopted for allocating trading quotas, whether positive pricing will be implemented during allocation, how the price will be determined, and how sectoral allocations will be specified are all of critical importance to the success of the system. Moreover, sectoral variability and firm participation are also essential for the structuring of the system. On the other hand, control mechanisms based on taxation cause rigidities between direct producers and end users and may adversely influence the decisions of market agents. Furthermore, relatively high taxes in Turkey, which are also incorporated in the financial regulations on environmental protection, do not successfully achieve meaningful reductions in CO_2 emissions. The results obtained show that the high-taxation policy adopted by Turkey has failed to bring about considerable progress in the reduction of CO_2 emissions.

The main source of the problem is that, despite taxation, there has been a failure to develop alternative sources to the energy-intensive resource-inefficient polluting processes. In cases where substitutes for polluting industrial processes are not developed, the only outcomes of high taxation are increased production costs and increased revenues for the treasury, with no meaningful success in environmental pollution reduction.

Efforts to realize emission reduction through MBMs are under global discussion under the topic of "emission trading." Functioning on both compulsory and voluntary bases, this system seeks to measure GHG emissions generated by economic activities (in terms of carbon equivalents), price these emissions, make countries adopt or espouse them through quotas, and thus facilitate carbon trading at a global level. The ultimate aim is to incite actors to embrace GHG emission costs, known as externalities, and encourage them to use clean efficiency-improving technologies and thereby reduce their emissions.

REFERENCES

Acar, S., Challe, S., Christopoulos, S., Christo, G., 2014. Fossil Fuel Subsidies as a Lose-Lose: Fiscal and Environmental Burdens in Turkey. Presented at the 14th IAEE European Energy Conference, Rome, Italy, 28–31 October.

Acar, S., Kitson, L., Bridle, R., 2015. Subsidies to Coal and Renewable Energy in Turkey. Global Subsidies Initiative Report. IISD, March.

Acar, S., Yeldan, E., 2016. Environmental impacts of coal subsidies in Turkey: a general equilibrium analysis. Energy Policy 90, 1–15. doi: 10.1016/j.enpol.2015.12.003.

Ari, İ., Sari, R., 2015. The role of feed-in tariffs in emission mitigation: Turkish case. Renewable Sustain. Energy Rev 48, 768–775. doi: 10.1016/j.rser.2015.04.006.

Baris, K., Kucukali, S., 2012. Availability of renewable energy sources in Turkey: current situation, potential, government policies and the EU perspective. Energy Policy 42, 377–391.

Benli, H., 2013. Potential of renewable energy in electrical energy production and sustainable energy development of Turkey: performance and policies. Renewable Energy 50, 33–46.

Bridle, R., Kitson, L., 2014. The Impact of Fossil-Fuel Subsidies on Renewable Electricity Generation. International Institute for Sustainable Development (IISD)—Global Subsidies Initiative (GSI), Report, Available from: https://www.iisd.org/gsi/sites/default/files/ffs_rens_impacts.pdf.

Herdem Attorneys at Law, 2013. Turkey Energy Report. Available from: http://www.herdem.av.tr/resimler_site/2013_TURKEY_ENERGY_REPORT_FINAL.pdf.

International Energy Agency (IEA), 2013a. Tracking Clean Energy Progress 2013: IEA Input to the Clean Energy Ministerial. OECD/IEA, Paris, France, Available from: http://www.iea.org/publications/TCEP_web.pdf.

International Energy Agency (IEA), 2013b. Turkey Oil and Gas Security: Emergency Responses of IEA Countries. OECD, Paris, France.
International Energy Agency (IEA), 2016. Energy Policies of IEA Countries: Turkey. Available from http://www.oecd-ilibrary.org/energy/energy-policies-of-iea-countries_19900082.
MEU, September 27, 2016. Karbon Piyasalarına Hazırlık Ortaklığı Projesi Emisyon Ticaret Sisteminin Türkiye'ye Uygunluğunun Değerlendirilmesi Bileşeni Son Çalıştayları, Ek Dosyalar. Available from: https://www.csb.gov.tr/projeler/iklim/index.php?Sayfa=habe rdetay&Id=64883.
Ren21, 2013. Renewable Energy Policy Network for the 21th Century. Renewables 2013 Global Status Report. Available from: http://www.ren21.net/REN21Activities/GlobalStatusReport.aspx.
Republic of Turkey, 2005. Law on Utilization of RES for the Purpose of Generating Electrical Energy. Available from: http://www.eie.gov.tr/eie-web/english/announcements/YEK_kanunu/LawonRenewableEnergyReources.pdf.
Republic of Turkey, 2009a. Electricity Energy Market and Supply Security Strategy Paper.
Schreiber, H., 2004. Risk Sharing and Renewable Energy. The Case of Geothermal Energy Projects. International Geothermal Days, Zakopane, Poland, September 13-17.
Turhan, E., Mazlum, S.C., Şahin, Ü., Şorman, A.H., Gündoğan, A.C., 2016. Beyond special circumstances: climate change policy in Turkey 1992–2015. WIREs Clim. Change 7 (3), 448–460.
Turkish Electricity Transmission Company (TEIAS), 2013. Turkish Electricity Production Planning Study (2005–2020). Available from: http://www.teias.gov.tr/Eng/apkuretimplani/veriler.htm#_Toc86219420.
UNFCCC, 2016. Aggregate effect of the intended nationally determined contributions: an update, Synthesis report by the secretariat, Advanced version, FCCC/CP/2016/2, 2 May 2016, http://unfccc.int/resource/docs/2016/cop22/eng/02.pdf.
United Nations. Economic Commission for Africa. Subregional Office West Africa (SRO-WA) (2013-03). Inclusive green growth to accelerate socio-economic development in West Africa. UN. ECA Intergovernmental Committee of Experts (16th ICE) of West Africa (16th session: March 2013: Abidjan, CÔTE D'IVOIRE). http://hdl.handle.net/10855/22124.
Yuksel, I., 2013. Renewable energy status of electricity generation and future prospect hydropower for Turkey. Renewable Energy 50, 1037–1043.

FURTHER READING

Doukas, A., Acar, S., 2015. G20 Subsidies to Oil, Gas and Coal Production: Turkey. Background Paper to the report Empty Promises: G20 Subsidies to Oil, Gas and Coal Production. Jointly prepared by the IISD, OCI and ODI.
IEA, 2010. Deploying Renewables in Southeast Asia: Trends and Potentials.
MVV Consultants and Engineers GmbH, 2004. Energy Efficiency Strategy for Turkey. Berlin, Germany. Available from: http://www.eie.gov.tr/eie-web/TK%20EE%20strategy%20-%20revised_04062004.pdf.
Republic of Turkey, 2009b. Republic of Turkey Ministry of Energy and Natural Resources Strategic Plan (2010–2014). Available from: http://www.enerji.gov.tr/yayinlar_raporlar_EN/ETKB_2010_2014_Stratejik_Plani_EN.pdf.
UNFCCC, 2013. National Greenhouse Gas Inventory Data for the period 1990–2011. Available from: http://unfccc.int/resource/docs/2013/sbi/eng/19.pdf.
Yeldan, et al., 2016. Ekonomi Politikaları Perspektifinden İklim Değişikliği ile Mücadele. TÜSİAD- T/2016 T/2016,12 – 583.

CHAPTER 4

Modeling for Green Growth: Environmental Policy in a Dualistic Peripheral Economy

The main methodological apparatus of this study is now introduced. The overall characteristics of this quantitative and analytical approach and initially introduced, and its salient features are discussed in contrast to alternative modeling techniques that have been reported in the literature. This modeling framework rests on the theoretical basis of general equilibrium with various economic activities across many markets, as interplayed by diverse actors, households, producers, governmental bodies, and the foreign economy.

Thus the focus of this chapter is on the nature and consequences of the dynamic interplay of general equilibrium interactions. It is set within the context of structural characteristics of a developing economy (i.e., Turkey) to reveal regional stratification and duality. The analytical approach is based on the methodology of applied general equilibrium distinguished as the folklore of computable general equilibrium (CGE). The methodological rationale is based on the urgent need to improve understanding of the complex trade-offs between attaining sustainable development, mitigating the threat of climate change, and enhancing social welfare. The need to identify an analytical resolution for ranking alternative policy instruments and interactions from the point of view of social welfare and economic well-being will also be addressed.

The CGE modeling methodology is the most conducive analytical apparatus for capturing these diverse objectives and policy trade-offs within the discipline of general equilibrium theory. Embedded in the theoretical realm of the Walrasian equilibrium, the CGE framework provides a coherent system of data management and scenario analyses to simultaneously address issues of sustainability and mitigation.

The concept of developmental sustainability is a fairly recent phenomenon that came into development economics through the 1987 report of the *World Commission on Environment and Development* led by the *Brundtland Commission*. The Brundtland report succinctly summarized the concept as

Macroeconomics of Climate Change in a Dualistic Economy
http://dx.doi.org/10.1016/B978-0-12-813519-8.00004-2

"… development which meets the needs of the present without compromising the ability of future generations to meet their own needs." Sustainability has since become one of the most influential phrases of the environmental policy agenda.

Thus what is needed is a coherent analysis of the systemic relations surrounding the energy–economy–environment (3E) nexus. Thus the CGE framework is utilized as a social laboratory tool for addressing policy questions over the 3E realm.

4.1 THE CGE FOLKLORE

The CGE methodology is an applied approach to the Walrasian economic system. It is *Walrasian* in the sense that it brings behavioral assumptions, production technologies, and market institutions together within the discipline of general equilibrium. Along with equilibrium production processes, it also brings factors of production (i.e., capital, labor, and energy aggregate input) within a dynamically adjusting technological pathway.

Commensurate with production activities, incomes are generated through wages, profits, and other factor payments. Income remunerations are channeled to the households whose role in the system is to dispose of the generated factor income through (private) consumption expenditure on commodities or (private) savings. Saving funds are, in turn, disposed of as investment expenditures on fixed capital to accentuate the potential output in the next production cycle.

Following the identification of national income accounting, any gap in the domestic savings–investment balance is met by foreign savings; that is, the balance on the current account of the balance of payments. Adjustments on a flexible (real) exchange rate (conversion factor of the price indexes of domestically produced versus foreign goods), or quantity adjustments on foreign exchange flows, are possible modes to bring forth the warranted equilibrium. Governments are institutionalized in every aspect of economic activity considered thus far. Through the administration of taxation or subsidization, governments can act as economic agents to fulfil public expenditure or saving accounts, and function as administrative units to design alternative policy scenarios and implement instruments of abatement. The CGE framework has the capability to provide an economic evaluation of "what if?" policy interventions under various abatement scenarios.

Thus given their structural flexibility and theoretical consistency, CGE models have become standard tools for the quantitative analysis of policy inference by international agencies (i.e., the Organisation for Economic Co-operation and Development (OECD) and the World Bank) and numerous national bodies of developmental and environmental policy. Deeper surveys are provided by Bergman (1990), Bhattacharyya (1996), Böhringer and Löschel (2006), and Shoven and Whalley (1992).

Chapter 2 briefly discussed the basic dual-economy model and the models of structural transformation, building on the earlier works of Higgins (1956), Jorgenson (1961, 1966, 1967), Lewis (1954), and Ranis and Fei (1961). The CGE literature offers a sophisticated platform to study the basics of the dual-economy model, such as interdependencies among different sectors of the economy, productivity differences between modern and traditional sectors, patterns of unemployment and underemployment, labor market imperfections, and dynamics of (qualitatively) different types of growth-capital accumulation. With high levels of data disaggregation, CGE models also provide substantial gains in the move towards more realistic structures (de Melo, 1977; Sue Wing, 2004; Temple, 2005).

The reflection of the model on "modern sector dualism" puts considerable focus on labor market (or market) imperfections, of which the effects project onto the labor markets. Imperfect or segmented labor markets have implications for sectoral production structures, sectoral productivity differentials, and aggregate outcomes (Temple, 2004). Multisectoral CGE models are therefore useful, and required, in the analysis of interactions between urban unemployment, informal sector size, and structural transformation and economic growth patterns.

Understanding structural change and its determinants clearly has direct policy implications. Applied multisectoral general equilibrium models that provide detailed accounts of the economic structure in developing economies are often used to assess policy alternatives and have long-term impacts (i.e., climate change). These models offer a framework with multisectors, different production structures, detailed representations of the labor markets, possible migration dynamics, and regional specialization. They are also capable of providing modern accounts of the interactions between long-term structural transformation and the distribution of welfare. Hence CGE models with basic "dualistic" structures are extensively utilized to study inequality and poverty.

Representation of the well-documented features of the labor market in developing countries (i.e., wage efficiency, a large informal sector, labor market segmentation, a heterogeneous and imperfectly mobile labor force, and wage flexibility in the informal sector) allows these models to study the strong links between the structure of the labor markets, the transmission of policy shock, and inequality and poverty (Agénor, 2004). Many classical CGE models work with homogenous labor markets with a fixed supply of labor and flexible wages; however, the models that aim to analyze poverty and the poverty-reduction implications of policies (i.e., trade liberalization, structural adjustment, and social transference) engage in more detailed representation of the labor market, often accompanied with other dualistic attributes of developing economies.[1]

The representation of labor heterogeneity through the distinction between formal and informal and urban and rural labor under various degrees of substitution forms the basic approach for developing "dual labor market" structures in applied general equilibrium modeling (Graafland et al., 2001; Hendy and Zaki, 2013). The basic idea of the Harris and Todaro (1970) framework, which stated that urban–formal and rural–informal labor markets are not completely isolated from each other but are connected via (imperfect) labor mobility, has also been extensively utilized in CGE models studying poverty and inequality (Agénor et al., 2003; Alzua and Ruffo, 2011; Gilbert and Wahl, 2002; Yang and Huang, 1997).

The "dual–dual" structure adopted by Thorbecke (1993) not only uses the formal–informal labor characterization of these CGE models but further introduces coexisting modern and informal activities in both urban and rural areas, which is usually the case for typical middle-income developing economies (Khan, 2004). Stifel and Thorbecke (2003) provide an example model of an archetype African economy to simulate the welfare effects of trade liberalization on poverty. The presence of dualism (modern and informal activities) within each sector makes it possible to analyze the distribution of both activities in rural and urban areas. Hence the single modeling framework captures a subsistence agriculture using traditional labor-intensive technologies, a large-scale capital-intensive agriculture producing mostly export goods, the urban–informal sector, and the urban–modern sector.[2]

---

[1] Boeters and Savard (2012) provide a detailed review of alternatives for modeling labor markets in CGE models.

[2] Khan (2004) provides further discussion on the characteristics of applied general equilibrium models for poverty policy analysis in the context of developing countries. He emphasizes the importance of representing typical features including, market power, the role of intermediate and capital goods, the structure of financial systems, and the roles of labor markets and the informal sector.

Structuralist models, which focus on the role of demand to understand structural transformation, also provide examples of formal and informal production structures in developing economies. Rada and von Armin (2014) and Morrone (2016) performed studies in India and Brazil, respectively. They highlighted the existence of formal and informal production activities with differentiated productivity levels, and emphasized the role of the informal sector in supplying the reservoir of labor for understanding the complexity of structural transformation dynamics in a middle-income developing economy. In a different framework, Roson and van der Mensbrugghe (2017) emphasized the importance of distinguishing between the supply-side effects (which affect sectoral productivity and growth dynamics) and the demand-side effects (which capture the variations in the structure of final demand) for understanding structural transformation. Their results indicate that time-varying and income-dependent demand structures generate sizable variations in the industrial structure.

The relevance of regional modeling and regional CGE models in representing and analyzing the spatial distribution of "dualistic" structures, and the implications of such distributions on the structural transformation and geographical distribution of welfare in developing economies, should be noted. Regional and multiregional CGE models that emphasize the roles of the spatial distribution of production activities and (endogenous and imperfect) interregional migration contribute to our understanding of differentiated development paths. Many regional CGE modeling reviews are available; however, Donaghy (2009), Giesecke and Madden (2012), Kraybill (1993), and Partridge and Rickman (2010) provide the basis for understanding the effects of incorporating key regional features (i.e., regional labor markets and interregional migration) into structural transformation models.

The CGE approach is not the only method for quantitatively modeling the economics of climate change. A wide arsenal of quantitative methods exist to assess the complex set of interactions over the 3E nexus; however, a thorough survey is beyond the main focus of this study. Nevertheless, a brief synopsis of the alternative methods is instrumental in placing the CGE methodology in the right framework to emphasize its advantages and misconceptions.

The so-called macroeconometric models, mainly of Keynesian tradition, have close affinity with the CGE model. These models rely on large datasets, often with long time series, and are amenable to statistical inference and probabilistic hypothesis testing. However, they typically fail to capture the cause–effect relationships between the economic machine and environmental pollution, and their analytical power at ranking the welfare implications of the policy instruments of abatement is rather limited. The CGE framework, with its theoretical basis laid out over the Walrasian general equilibrium foundation, can accommodate the structural cause–effect hypothesis over a wide range of behavioral motives and endogenous market signals. Furthermore, with their ability to make "what if?" assessments against a "business-as-usual" trajectory, their simulation exercises offer a viable metric for ranking the cause–effect impact of alternative policy regimes that combat climate change and mitigation.

Conversely, the nature of CGEs means that they can accommodate energy sector activities through their production functions and characterize economic behavior in response to the cost minimization impulses of "rational agents." The CGE apparatus typically only addresses the workings of the energy system through the cost-value system of economic relations and, as such, may fail to provide sharp flows of the technical aspects of energy production and distribution.

An alternative take on the technical attributes of the energy system is accomplished by the bottom–up approach of modeling. In contrast to the top-down CGE analysis, the bottom–up models attempt to capture the technical nature of the substitution possibilities and input requirements across the primary and final sources of energy production and distribution. They focus exclusively on substitution and input requirements to produce a given energy throughput. As the cheapest method of energy substitutes, they attempt to offer the most efficient energy production technique that would indirectly serve as abatement projections.

However, a major deficiency of bottom–up methods is their lack of ability to address energy–economy interactions. In particular, working typically within the constraints of fixed final demands, they do not accommodate feedback mechanisms from the economy to the energy system. In addition, they fail to offer much on the warranted implications of the policy instruments on the rate of growth, employment, and the path of capital investments (the rebound effect).

However, it should be noted that this arguably diverse dichotomy does not necessarily pertain to a theoretical departure, but in the words of Böhringer and Löschel (2006, p. 50) it may "…simply relate to the level of aggregation and scope of ceteris paribus assumptions." There have been various attempts to merge both approaches within a megaframework, embedding the bottom–up energy module with the Walrasian general equilibrium system of the simultaneous equations of a CGE (Böhringer, 1998; Manne, 1981).

Therefore there is not a single all-encompassing methodology. Starting with the general equilibrium theory for the socially-efficient instruments of abatement under informalization and duality within the context of the Turkish economy applied here, more steps ought to be investigated to advance our understanding of the complex dynamics between economy, society, and the environment.

4.1.1 Modeling the 3E Nexus via CGE Analytics

The version of the CGE model utilized in this study uses various methods to address the characteristic features of peripheral development and the dual objectives of development and environmental abatement. One distinguishing feature of the current model is that it deliberately recognizes regional differentiation in employment and production to accommodate the traps of poverty and technological backwardness. Turkey can be used as a viable example of a peripheral economy with a key mandate for sustaining energy sufficiency and generating growth and employment. However, the country is currently facing strong international pressure to bring its gaseous emissions under control. These constitute the main traits of the Turkey CGE model to be utilized in this study.

The model also takes account of the rigidities in the labor and capital markets by introducing explicit gaps against the equalization of the wage and profit rates across sectors. These "distortions" are set from the existing data on wage rates (and profit rates) across sectors, and are maintained as rigid divergences from equalization of the "average" wage rate. Migration is a further behavioral rule, which governs the movement of labor from poor regions (and its sectors) towards the affluent high-wage sectors of the high-income regions.

Environmental damage is mainly modeled in the form of gaseous pollution. Greenhouse gas emissions (measured as CO_2 equivalents) are thought to be the end result of four sets of economic activities: (1) the combustion of fossil fuels to produce aggregate energy; (2) industrial processes used for the production of iron, steel, chemicals, and cement; (3) agricultural processes (mainly methane); and (4) household consumption and waste.

Submodeling of environmental pollution in the CGE apparatus recognizes these sources using technological parameters derived from the CO_2 eq. emissions inventory published by TurkStat. A bird's-eye view of these relationships is portrayed in Fig. 4.1. Pollution is documented across the

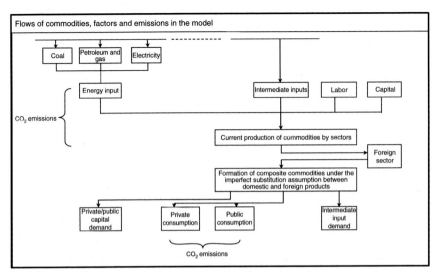

Figure 4.1 *Structure of emission flow under general equilibrium.*

energy-production activities and industrial and agricultural processes within the given production technologies. Waste is generated through consumption activities of private households.

The CGE methodology accommodates these activities by selecting the free parameters to fit the algebraic equation system to the base-year equilibrium data, a procedure known as *calibration*. Calibration involves compilation of an annual dataset (in equilibrium) across its expenditures and revenues. Tabulated as a micro- and macrosystem of equilibrium relationships, this dataset is referred to as the social accounting matrix (SAM) (Pyatt and Round (1979) provide a seminal introduction to the SAM system of accounts). The model's algebraic specifications are then utilized to distill the parametric values including the share parameters on production and consumption, key shift variables of numerous functional forms, and policy rates (i.e., taxes and subsidies). The "calibrated" model must be able to generate the original dataset disclosed in the SAM without any further statistical inference. This solution is known as the "base year." Using a set of behavioral rules of capital accumulation and technical change alongside exogenous labor force (population) growth, dynamic CGE simulations set the stage for a *base path*.

The CGE exercises in this model will utilize the 2012 input–output (I/O) flow data published by TurkStat. Starting from the base year (2012), the algebraic system of general equilibrium will be accommodated by calibrating the free parameters and shift variables as noted above.

The algebraic equations are introduced in a more formal format in the following section, which documents our data in the SAM system.

4.2 ALGEBRAIC STRUCTURE OF THE CGE MODEL

The model is composed of 17 production sectors spanning two regionalied bodies for the Turkish economy (*high* versus *low income*), a representative private household to carry out savings-consumption decisions, a government to implement public policies towards environmental abatement, and a "rest of the world" account to resolve the balance of payment transactions. Antecedents of the model rest on the seminal contributions of the CGE analyses on gaseous pollutants, energy utilization, and climate change economics for Turkey as shown in Acar and Yeldan (2016), Kumbaroglu (2003), Lise (2006), Akin-Ölçüm and Yeldan (2013), Şahin (2004), Telli et al. (2008), and Vural (2009); however, it should be noted that these studies were based on *national* aggregates. Given the official focus on regional investment and subsidization in Turkey, it is pertinent to work with a regional diversification. Such an exercise was implemented in Yeldan et al. (2013, 2014) in the context of duality of *middle income* versus *poverty traps* of the Turkish socioeconomic structure. This procedure is followed here for the compilation of regional-level data. More details of this procedure are given Section 4.2.3.

4.2.1 Commodity Structure and Regional Commodity Markets

In the absence of official *regional* I/O data for this model, the procedure of Yeldan et al. (2013, 2014) in setting a regional differentiation of the components of final demand was followed. Aggregate national accounts were decomposed into two regions: *high and low income*. This decomposition was used to generate a "final goods aggregate" of macroeconomic demand based on product differentiation and imperfect substitution, as in Armington (1969). The *Armingtonian composite* goods structure was utilized in setting the demand for the domestically produced goods versus imports of total absorption ($Q^S + M - X$). This notion was extended across regions, and the sectorial domestically produced goods aggregate (DC_i) was decomposed into the regional sources (as shown in Eq. (4.1)):

$$DC_i = BC_i \left[\gamma_i DC_{i,RH}^{-\rho_i} + (1-\gamma_i) DC_{i,RL}^{-\rho_i} \right]^{-1/\rho_i} \tag{4.1}$$

Thus $DC_{i,R}$ ($R = RH, RL$) forms the aggregate domestic goods along an imperfect substitution specification of the Armington aggregate. The aggregate composite goods (absorption) were then given as a constant elasticity of substitution (CES) aggregation of imports (M_i) and DC_i (as shown in Eq. (4.2)):

$$CC_i = AC_i \left[\delta i DC_i^{-\phi_i} + (1 - \delta_i) M_i^{-\phi_i} \right]^{-1/\phi_i} \tag{4.2}$$

Production activities were differentiated using regional data on production, employment, and exports.

4.2.2 Production Technology and Gaseous Pollutants

The production of gross output was modeled as a multistage activity of nested production function in each sector (i). At the top-stage gross output of region R, sector i was given by an expanded CES functional of the form:

$$Q_{i,R}^S = A_{i,R} \left[\gamma VA_{i,R}^{-\beta_i} + (1 - \gamma_i) E_{i,R}^{-\beta_i} \right]^{-1/\beta_i} \tag{4.3}$$

In Eq. (4.3), A denotes exogenously determined total factor productivity (TFP), VA is the sectorial value added, and E is the energy aggregate input. Thus the aggregate output supply brings together the value-added component with the energy input requirement of the sector. The energy aggregate input was assumed to be utilized in the sectorial gross output production only imperfectly substituting the value-added activities. This elasticity of substitution is given as $\left(\dfrac{1}{1 - \beta} \right)$.

In Eq. (4.4) VA is obtained via the conventional Cobb–Douglas specification of the two major factors of production; capital (K) and labor aggregate (LA).

$$VA_{i,R} = K_{i,R}^{\lambda_K} LA_{i,R}^{\lambda_{LA}} \tag{4.4}$$

Here LA is the labor aggregate of two types of labor recognized in the model: formal and informal (vulnerable). Eq. (4.5) shows a composition of labor aggregates where formal and informal labor types substitute each other, albeit imperfectly, along CES formulations.

$$LA_{i,R} = A_{i,R}^L \left[\Lambda_{i,R} LF_{i,R}^{-\eta_{i,R}} + (1 - \Lambda_{i,R}) LI_{i,R}^{-\eta_{i,R}} \right]^{-1/\eta_{i,R}} \tag{4.5}$$

Each sector uses intermediate inputs $(IN_{j,i})$ derived from the I/O data. In Eq. (4.6) the variable E denotes the energy composite aggregate comprised of three environmentally sensitive activities of energy generation: coal (CO), petroleum and gas (PG), and electricity (EL). At the lower end of the two-stage characterization of sectorial output, this energy composite is determined by a CES function of its components:

$$E_{i,R} = A_{i,R}^E \left[\varphi_{CO,i,R} IN_{CO,i,R}^{-\rho_{i,R}} + \varphi_{PG,i,R} IN_{PG,i,R}^{-\rho_{i,R}} + \varphi_{EL,i,R} IN_{EL,i,R}^{-\rho_{i,R}} \right]^{-1/\rho_{i,R}} \quad (4.6)$$

Under the given energy production technology, the optimum mix of inputs of CO, PG, and EL is determined by equating their marginal rate of technical substitution to their respective (input) prices, as affected by possible fiscal policy:

$$\frac{IN_{CO,i,R}}{IN_{EL,i,R}} = \left[\left(\frac{\varphi_{CO,i,R}}{1 - \varphi_{CO,i,R} - \varphi_{PG,i,R}} \right) \left(\frac{P_{EL,i,R}}{\left(1 + t_{CO,i,R}^{ENV}\right) P_{CO,i,R}} \right) \right]^{\sigma_{i,R}} \quad (4.7)$$

$$\frac{IN_{PG,i,R}}{IN_{EL,i,R}} = \left[\left(\frac{\varphi_{PG,i,R}}{1 - \varphi_{CO,i,R} - \varphi_{PG,i,R}} \right) \left(\frac{P_{EL,i,R}}{\left(1 + t_{PG,i,R}^{ENV}\right) P_{PG,i,R}} \right) \right]^{\sigma_{i,R}} \quad (4.8)$$

In Eqs. (4.7) and (4.8) t^{ENV} is the relevant tax instrument on the pollutant activity and σ is the elasticity of substitution with $\sigma = 1/(1 + \rho)$.

Sectorial demands for capital and labor follow the conventional optimization rules for equating marginal products with their respective input prices. The production technology for value added in Eq. (4.4) is of constant returns, thus Eq. (4.9) is used:

$$\lambda_{K,i,R} + \lambda_{LA,i,R} = 1 \quad (4.9)$$

The aggregate CO_2 emissions were captured in each sector (and region) from three origins: primary energy combustion (EE), secondary energy combustion (SE), and industrial processes (IND). In this specification, SE was due to the utilization of refined petroleum (RP), and emissions from IND were derived exclusively from iron and steel (IS), chemicals (CH), and cement (CE). The aggregate energy material balance data were used to map each sector's CO_2 emissions to these major sources using the summary in Table 4.1.

Distinct mechanisms were specified depending on the source of origin of the gaseous CO_2 eq. emissions. Emissions from EE activities were captured using Eq. (4.10), and emissions from SE of RP were captured using Eq. (4.11).

$$CO_{2EE}^{j,i,R} = \varepsilon_{j,i,R} \, a_{j,i,R} \, Q_{j,i,R}^S \quad (4.10)$$

$$CO_{2SE}^{RP,i,R} = z_{RP,i,R} \, a_{RP,i,R} \, Q_{RP,i,R}^S \quad (4.11)$$

Table 4.1 Distribution of CO_2 emissions from sectoral production activities by their source of origin

Abbreviations	Sectoral producers	Industrial processes	Primary energy utilization	Secondary energy utilization
AG	Agriculture	0.00	0.00	1.00
CO	Coal	0.00	0.30	0.70
PG	Crude oil and natural gas	0.00	0.80	0.20
PE	Refined petroleum	0.00	0.88	0.12
CE	Cement	0.66	0.16	0.18
IS	Iron and steel	0.67	0.15	0.18
MW	Machinery and white goods	0.00	0.00	1.00
ET	Electronics	0.00	0.75	0.25
AU	Auto industry	0.00	0.30	0.70
EL	Electricity production	0.00	1.00	0.00
CN	Construction	0.00	0.00	1.00
OE	Other economy	0.00	0.40	0.60

Source: Adopted from Energy Balances Tables, Min of Energy, and Natural Resources.

The parameter $\varepsilon_{j,i,R}$ in Eq. (4.10) summarizes the energy use coefficients (calibrated from the material energy balances tables) to set the composition of emissions from primary energy via the combustion of CO and PG in each sector. The $z_{RP,i,R}$ parameter in Eq. (4.11) similarly represents the emission coefficient due to the combustion of RP. The traditional I/O coefficient, $a_{j,i} = \dfrac{IN_{j,i}}{Q_i^S}$, is responsive to price signals via optimizating costs, given technology (4.3). This is in contrast to traditional CGE analyses where $a_{j,i}$ is typically regarded as fixed, as in a Leontieff technology.

Emissions from IND were recognized from IS, CH, and CE. These emissions were regarded as proportional to their respective real output (as shown in Eq. (4.12)):

$$CO_{2i,R}^{IND} = \eta_{i,R} Q_{i,R}^S \quad i \in \{IS, CH, CE\} \tag{4.12}$$

Emissions from agricultural processes were similarly set proportionally to agricultural gross outputs. Emissions of non-CO_2 gasses (CH_4, F, and NO_2) were set proportionally to the EE activities. Thus CO_2 eq. emissions of CH_4 were calculated as shown in Eq. (4.13) and CH_4 from waste was calculated as per Eq. (4.14).

$$CO_{2CH_4}^{j,i,R} = \varepsilon_{j,i,R}\ a_{j,i,R}\ Q_{i,R}^S \quad \text{for } j = \{CO, PG\} \tag{4.13}$$

$$CO_{2WST}^{j,i,R} = \varpi_{j,i,R}\ Q_{i,R}^S \tag{4.14}$$

Household demand for energy generates an additional source of CO_2 eq. emissions. This was regarded as proportional to the household consumption of basic fuels (CO and RP) and calculated as in Eq. (4.15):

$$CO_2^{HH} = \sum_{i \in CO,RP} K_i C_i^D \tag{4.15}$$

Aggregate CO_2 eq. emissions were calcualted as the sum of each of these sources (as shown in Eq. (4.16)):

$$\begin{aligned}
CO_2^{TOT} = \sum_{j,i,R}\Big(CO_{2j,i,R}^{EE} + CO_{2j,i,R}^{SE} + CO_{2j,i,R}^{CH_4} + CO_{2j,i,R}^{WST} +\Big) \\
+ \sum_{i \in IS,CE} CO_{2i,R}^{IND} + \sum_R CO_{2R}^{AGR} + CO_2^{HH}
\end{aligned} \tag{4.16}$$

4.2.3 Labor Markets, Income Generation, and General Equilibrium

The model distinguishes two types of labor: urban (formal) and informal. The formal wage rate is fixed and the formal labor market adjusts with unemployment in each period. The flexibility of the real wage in the informal labor market is characterized by the extent of fragmentation across the dualistic labor market in the Turkish economy. Data from different sectors and labor types were compiled from various TurkStat data sources. TurkStat provides sectoral labor employment data at the Nace Rev. 2 four-digit level, and regional formal–informal employment disaggregation data for the major sectors (i.e., agriculture, industry, and services) at the NUTS-2 level. The comprehensive treatment of both datasets makes it possible to approximate the sectoral formal and informal employment figures for both regions. In addition, the household labor force surveys (HLFS) from TurkStat were also used to determine the sectoral formal and informal wage ratios for the Nace Rev. 2, level 1. Hence total employment and total payments were obtained for each labor category in each region to enable calibration of the necessary parameters of the labor market.

The formal labor market was hypothesized to clear by quantity adjustments on employment (as shown in Eq. (4.17)):

$$U_{LF,R} = L_{LF,R}^S - \sum_i LF_{i,R}^D \tag{4.17}$$

Conversely, the informal or vulnerable labor market operates with fully flexible wages. The low level of informal wages is a symptomatic proxy for poverty in the informal labor market.

The regional labor markets have been linked by migration over time. This is based on (expected) wage differences between high- and low–income Turkey, and is driven along the classic Harris and Todaro (1970) specification. Given the migrants from each labor type (l):

$$\text{MIG}_l(t) = \mu_l \left[\frac{\left(E\left[W_{l,\text{RH}}\right] - W_{l,\text{RL}} \right)}{W_{l,\text{RL}}} \right] L^S_{l,\text{RL}} \qquad (4.18)$$

where $E[W_{l,\text{RH}}]$ is the expected wage rate of labor type l (=LF, LI) in the high-income region and μ_l is a calibration parameter (as shown in Eq. (4.18)).

Given that $\text{MIG}_l(t)$ is based on wage expectations from high-income regions, labor supplies evolve according to Eq. (4.19):

$$L^S_{l,\text{RL}}(t+1) = \left(1 + n_{l,\text{RL}}\right) L^S_{l,\text{RL}}(t) - \text{MIG}_l(t)$$
$$L^S_{l,\text{RH}}(t+1) = \left(1 + n_{l,\text{RH}}\right) L^S_{l,\text{RH}}(t) + \text{MIG}_l(t) \qquad (4.19)$$

Capital stocks evolve given the net of depreciation of fixed investments. The allocation of aggregate net investment funds to specific sectors (investment by destination sector) is accomplished through the calculation of regional profitability. Given sectorial profit rates ($r_{i,R}$) across regions, and the economy-wide average profit rate (r^{AVG}), sectorial investment allocations ($\Delta K_{i,R}(t+1)$) are given by the simple rule in Eq. (4.20):

$$\Delta K_{i,R}(t+1) = \Pi_{i,R} + \Pi_{i,R} \left[\frac{r_{i,R} - r^{\text{AVG}}}{r_{i,R}} \right] \qquad (4.20)$$

where $\Pi_{i,R}$ is the share of aggregate profits in sector, i, and region, R. This sets the allocation of physical investments to be reused via profit differences in the second part of the equation.

Private household income is composed of wage incomes from labor and remittances of profits from the enterprise sector. Public sector revenues comprise tax revenues (i.e., from wage and capital incomes) and nontaxation sources of income (i.e., from various exogenous flows). The income flow of the public sector is further augmented by indirect taxes and environmental taxes. This model closely follows the fiscal budget constraints. Given public earnings, the government's "transfer expenditures to households" were adjusted endogenously to sustain other components of public demand (i.e., public investment and consumption expenditure) as fixed ratios to the national income.

General equilibrium of the system was obtained via endogenous solutions on prices, wage rates, and the exchange rate. Informal wage rates across regions clear regional labor markets. The balance of payments is cleared through flexible adjustments on the real exchange rate (the ratio of the price of domestic goods to imports in the CGE folklore), while the *nominal* conversion factor across domestic and world prices serves as the *numeraire* of the system.

The model was solved iteratively by updating the annual "solutions" of the model to 2030. Aggregate output supplies grew through three channels: (1) the exogenous growth of labor supplies; (2) investments on physical capital net of depreciation; and (3) TFP growth, which in turn was regarded as exogenous. Capital stocks across regions and sectors were augmented with net investments in each period. Regional labor supplies were increased exogenously by population growth and migration (see Eq. (4.18)). TFP rates were updated in a Hicks–neutral manner, and formal real wage rates were updated by the cost of living index (endogenously solved).

4.3 DATA SOURCES AND CALIBRATION METHODOLOGY

4.3.1 Construction of the Regional Social Accounting Database

Regional I/O data are not available in Turkey, and the most recent I/O data was tabulated in 2012 by TurkStat. Given the lack of official regional data, regional economic activities were differentiated based on the standard tools of CGE applications. The SAM for 2012 (published by TurkStat) was generated using national income data on macroaggregates. Labor remunerations were obtained from the International Labor Organization (ILO) and TurkStat HLFS data. The aggregated I/O table for 2012 is displayed in Table 4.2.

Following production of the regional SAM (available upon request), the national macroaggregates were decomposed via the shares of gross regional value added. Based on the differentiation of *level 2* NACE-1 data, 7 regions

Table 4.2 Turkey: I/O flow, 2012 (thousand TRY, at basic prices)

(a)

	AG	CO	PG-OM	PE	CH	CE	IS	PA	FD
AG: Agriculture	29,438,100.0	78,743.9	54,546.9	342.8	627,218.4	29,432.2	1,626.7	329,948.4	56,673,900.0
CO: Coal	241,156.8	1,812,815.0	46,806.7	0.0	51,800.0	1,212,684.0	9,904.6	5,596.6	11,085.5
PG-OM: Crude petrol, gas, and other mining	210,906.6	7,552.8	79,146.8	31,949,853.4	2,421,500.3	6,996,719.6	9,773,476.0	262,898.8	828,376.9
PE: Petroleum products and chemicals	4,463,786.0	482,505.4	1,413,983.2	896,789.5	881,275.0	1,805,806.0	404,557.2	103,165.7	655,855.6
CH: Chemicals	8,943,774.0	149,786.5	518,011.9	34,323.7	39,930,000.0	2,138,284.0	2,203,785.0	3,010,425.0	5,654,674.0
CE: Cement	131,181.1	29,774.1	176,995.1	959.4	638,264.6	6,899,405.0	404,325.4	4,348.3	551,646.0
IS: Iron and steel	6,189.1	176,973.1	189,257.0	15,557.3	628,560.3	402,435.3	22,077,700.0	128,280.6	110,110.1
PA: Paper and print	112,492.8	1,145.2	7,790.0	33,263.3	1,001,410.0	532,824.6	236,644.8	7,671,507.0	2,493,897.0
FD: Food processing	6,367,557.0	1,287.7	35,888.5	8,423.0	163,603.6	35,275.8	15,534.0	120,936.4	23,837,200.0
TE: Textiles and clothing	109,045.8	34,191.3	71,756.1	3,727.0	660,675.7	191,847.4	60,557.2	440,838.4	310,247.9
MW: Machinery and white goods	191,484.4	95,966.7	286,033.5	28,047.8	750,545.5	201,658.7	721,510.2	55,299.5	711,785.0
ET: Electronics	71,891.1	57,314.0	29,347.2	8,154.9	130,570.8	137,281.9	33,310.1	43,219.4	116,673.8
AU: Automotive	265,689.5	452.6	9,533.1	24.4	1,025.7	17,526.2	0.0	1,466.0	533.3
EL: Electricity	902,509.1	245,169.5	734,655.4	26,902.8	2,034,290.0	2,554,476.0	4,387,732.0	528,733.6	1,835,289.0
CN: Construction	364,064.3	41,899.8	51,341.5	2,076.5	226,323.2	85,032.7	254,640.8	44,775.1	350,386.1
TR: Transportation	2,578,411.0	245,772.3	1,498,623.4	862,801.3	3,252,146.0	1,882,996.0	4,523,179.0	1,073,265.0	7,004,565.0
OE: Other economy	7,502,169.0	619,327.6	3,218,933.1	1,689,206.0	11,925,900.0	6,085,395.0	31,673,200.0	4,342,108.0	20,183,500.0
Totals									
Compensation of employees	3,194,349.0	2,931,077.0	2,350,736.8	490,184.0	9,417,064.0	6,014,431.0	4,865,445.0	2,898,136.0	13,409,100.0
Gross payments to capital	114,385,806.7	7,537,819.5	6,476,128.0	4,300,537.1	26,692,027.6	13,138,833.8	17,346,494.5	6,496,242.2	44,601,389.6
Net taxes	−409,801.0	392,980.3	1,013,682.7	5,347,046.8	4,198,528.4	1,941,986.2	4,545,101.4	993,550.4	1,464,525.4
Total value added (at market prices)	117,170,354.7	10,861,876.9	9,840,547.5	10,137,767.9	40,307,620.0	21,095,251.0	26,757,040.9	10,387,928.7	59,475,015.0
Total production Exp	179,070,762.3	14,942,554.4	18,263,196.8	45,698,220.9	105,632,729.2	52,304,331.3	103,538,723.8	28,554,740.4	180,804,740.2

(b)

	Private consumption expenditure	Government consumption expenditure	Gross fixed capital formation
AG: Agriculture	70,943,213.9	0.0	10,984,631.9
CO: Coal	6,163,732.6	0.0	523,308.1
PG-OM: Crude petrol, gas, and other mining	0.0	0.0	0.0
PE: Petroleum products and chemicals	8,170,146.6	0.0	0.0
CH: Chemicals	15,741,170.2	14,653,682.7	276,625.2
CE: Cement	2,852,345.6	0.0	801,269.3
IS: Iron and steel	0.0	0.0	0.0
PA: Paper and print	4,908,205.9	0.0	0.0
FD: Food processing	116,848,603.9	0.0	0.0
TE: Textiles and clothing	55,215,191.4	0.0	372,594.0
MW: Machinery and white goods	3,885,275.6	0.0	59,032,407.9
ET: Electronics	17,821,133.8	0.0	22,081,839.7
AU: Automotive	17,253,690.8	0.0	21,843,085.3
EL: Electricity	24,604,258.9	0.0	0.0
CN: Construction	2,059,032.5	8,665.4	241,179,412.4
TR: Transportation	101,554,459.4	913,471.0	6,702,682.1
OE: Other economy	531,047,583.0	207,825,882.9	80,484,489.1
	979,068,044.0	**223,401,702.0**	**444,282,345.0**

TE	MW	ET	AU	EL	CN	TR	OE	Total intermediate exp
5,963,512.0	6,837.4	7,643.8	13.3	218.1	114,145.0	14,755.5	6,983,250.0	100,324,234.4
39,119.1	10,533.4	2,043.2	17,471.2	2,892,929.0	150,131.4	369,767.5	3,420,575.0	10,294,419.0
1,049,632.2	189,652.8	131,751.2	132,587.2	25,263,600.0	4,752,312.0	48,579.8	342,494.6	84,441,041.0
393,888.5	392,764.6	434,782.5	104,590.8	402,526.5	4,985,364.0	27,820,300.0	15,290,800.0	60,932,740.5
11,970,200.0	2,063,803.0	3,963,530.0	2,521,522.0	74,998.0	9,011,344.0	2,505,050.0	19,249,500.0	113,943,011.0
34,853.0	486,955.6	395,805.1	499,281.2	130,407.6	26,354,700.0	873,664.8	6,311,453.0	43,924,019.4
35,588.7	23,231,400.0	9,206,265.0	7,382,780.0	71,908.0	25,127,300.0	214,117.1	6,893,704.0	95,898,125.6
1,138,633.0	375,728.6	416,025.6	91,823.0	76,001.1	158,535.2	493,570.0	12,457,800.0	27,299,091.1
532,843.7	53,060.9	22,277.6	9,271.1	20,740.3	112,564.6	192,790.3	22,277,700.0	53,806,954.4
54,879,800.0	194,564.3	106,494.7	360,412.2	4,587.5	150,869.4	213,276.3	6,420,095.0	64,212,986.2
411,298.9	8,533,914.0	2,544,749.0	4,400,737.0	13,924.3	14,862,000.0	1,043,107.0	8,283,650.0	43,135,711.5
249,493.4	1,383,245.0	8,789,359.0	2,310,104.0	523,752.9	5,576,912.0	232,564.4	9,502,252.0	29,195,445.9
20.5	908,353.4	32,064.5	14,162,600.0	152.1	26,964.7	1,079,149.0	2,930,046.0	19,435,601.0
3,103,648.0	1,151,517.0	400,417.4	472,991.9	60,459,600.0	428,257.7	441,051.6	18,662,500.0	98,369,741.0
191,751.7	262,073.7	61,717.8	42,641.2	409,542.4	47,242,300.0	423,232.1	16,689,700.0	66,743,498.9
3,072,462.0	3,406,436.0	1,669,822.0	1,988,092.0	519,813.8	5,737,816.0	40,418,700.0	33,450,400.0	113,185,300.6
16,494,100.0	9,727,960.0	7,780,041.0	7,605,626.0	4,763,437.0	35,747,500.0	38,953,100.0	257,395,000.0	465,706,502.7
								1,490,848,424.1
19,660,200.0	11,817,200.0	5,591,437.0	5,157,910.0	3,486,053.0	28,437,900.0	17,995,900.0	300,861,000.0	438,578,122.8
40,845,650.7	25,534,769.8	11,112,743.6	11,235,858.0	18,247,251.3	96,009,108.4	106,232,907.8	495,482,442.8	1,045,676,011.6
2,564,477.7	2,551,131.5	2,102,840.6	2,389,320.9	5,542,117.9	7,227,473.0	16,871,035.3	26,681,983.0	85,417,980.6
63,070,328.4	39,903,101.3	18,807,021.2	18,783,088.9	27,275,422.2	131,674,481.4	141,099,843.1	823,025,425.8	**1,569,672,115.0**
162,631,173.1	92,281,901.0	54,771,810.6	60,885,633.0	122,903,560.8	312,213,497.4	256,436,618.5	1,269,586,345.4	**3,060,520,539.1**

Exports	Imports (−)	Total exp on value added	Total expenditure
10,924,038.1	14,105,355.9	78,746,527.9	179,070,762.3
9,371.6	2,048,276.9	4,648,135.4	14,942,554.4
6,053,357.1	72,231,201.2	−66,177,844.1	18,263,196.8
14,094,423.9	37,499,090.1	−15,234,519.6	45,698,220.9
27,660,558.7	66,642,318.8	−8,310,281.9	105,632,729.2
7,875,980.9	3,149,283.8	8,380,311.9	52,304,331.3
53,569,058.7	45,928,460.5	7,640,598.3	103,538,723.8
3,267,467.6	6,920,024.1	1,255,649.3	28,554,740.4
20,597,168.8	10,447,987.0	126,997,785.7	180,804,740.2
62,494,817.1	19,664,415.6	98,418,186.9	162,631,173.1
31,415,579.0	45,187,072.9	49,146,189.5	92,281,901.0
25,981,041.8	40,307,650.6	25,576,364.7	54,771,810.6
32,455,691.2	30,102,435.3	41,450,032.0	60,885,633.0
393,883.6	464,322.8	24,533,819.7	122,903,560.8
2,843,140.2	620,252.0	245,469,998.5	312,213,497.4
35,259,722.2	1,179,016.8	143,251,317.9	256,436,618.5
36,604,740.5	52,082,852.7	803,879,842.7	1,269,586,345.4
371,500,041.0	**448,580,017.0**	**1,569,672,115.0**	**3,060,520,539.1**

Table 4.3 Economic indicators across regions (million TRY, 2012)

Region	Gross regional value added	Employment of formal labor (thousand persons)	Employment of informal labor (thousand persons)	Regional exports	Taxes on production and employment
High-income[a]	1,099,689.6	11,054.9	6,111.7	295,561.4	138,472.5
Low-income[b]	296,848.9	3,517.8	4,136.6	75,938.6	34,661.1

[a] High-income regions: TR10, TR21, TR31, TR41, TR42, TR51, and TR61.
[b] Low-income regions: TR62, TR63, TR71, TR72, TR81, TR82, TR83, TR90, TR52, TR53, TR32, TR33, TR22, TRA1, TRB1, TRB2, TRC1, TRC2, and TRC3.
Source: Authors calculations from TurkStat, Regional National Income Statistics.

were distinguished as "high income" and 19 regions were classified as "low income." Data revealed that the low-income regions host approximately 60% of the total 73.7 million population, and produce around 32% of the aggregate value added. The remaining 68% of the aggregate value added originated in the *high-income* region. Further specifics of the regional macrodata are provided in Table 4.3.

The SAM tabulates the microlevel I/O data with the aggregate macrodata on public sector balances and resolves the saving–investment equilibrium. The latter discloses a current account deficit (foreign savings) of TRY 86,135.6 million (roughly 6.5% to the GDP). *High-* versus *low-income* Turkey yield the production activities, while components of aggregate national demand were revealed using imperfect substitution in demand, and were calibrated through standard methods of the Armingtonian composite system.

This procedure was definitely a poor alternative to more direct approaches based on regionally-differentiated production structures. However, this requires *regional* I/O data and regional material balances. In the absence of official or independent regional data, the Armingtonian imperfect substitutability framework based on cost optimization was utilized.

It is of note that the specification here was designed to only capture the regionally-differentiated component of (investment) subsidization. Therefore it should not be regarded as a detailed structural characterization of the dualistic (fragmented) patterns of production attributable to the Turkish economy, which is an issue beyond the scope of this paper.

4.3.2 Parametrization of Gaseous Pollutants

A total of 447.45 million tons of CO_2 eq. were reportedly released in Turkey in 2012. TurkStat data distinguished this sum into four sources (million tons): energy combustion (264.8), industrial processes (41.8), agricultural processes (21.2), and waste (56.5). Using a different level of aggregation, emissions of CO_2, CH_4, N_2O, and F-gasses accounted for 363.1, 58.0, 21.1, and 5.2 million tons of this total, respectively.

To direct these data into sectorial sources of origin, TurkStat data reported to the UNFCCC inventory system was used. Where possible, original data on greenhouse gas source and sink categories were used to make direct connections between the sectors in the official dataset and the sectors distinguished in this model (i.e., agriculture, refined petroleum, cement, iron and steel, and electricity). The remaining unaccounted CO_2 emissions were allocated to the aggregate using the share of the sectorial intermediate input demand. This exercise yielded CO_2 eq. emissions across production sectors and other activities as shown in Table 4.4.

Data in Table 4.4 was initially used to calculate the total sectorial emissions, CO_{2i}^{TOT}. This sum was decomposed into three main sources of origin: emissions from EE, SE, and IND. This was performed using Table 4.1. Assuming $\pi_{s,i}$ ($s \in$ EE,SE,IND) is a typical element of Table 4.1, then:

$$CO_{2S,i} = \pi_{S,i} \cdot CO_{2i}^{TOT}$$

The coefficient $z_{RP,i}$ was subsequently calibrated by:

$$z_{RP,i} = \frac{CO_{2RP,i}^{SE}}{IN_{RP,i}}$$

For distinguishing this aggregate into the regional activities, regional shares of sectorial output were used. The source of CO_2 eq. emissions ideally ought to be used for regions; however, ad hoc specifications were not made due to the absence of precise regional data measurements. A similar procedure was followed to determine the EE sources of CO_2 eq. emissions across sectors (for $j \in$ CO and PG) and $CO_{2j,i}^{EE}$ was found from data displayed in Table 4.4 using the $\varepsilon_{j,i}$ for $j \in$ CO and PG.

4.3.3 Calibration of the Labor Markets

Two types of labor were distinguished in the model: formal and informal. The characterization was based on the ILOs definition of informal employ-

Table 4.4 Aggregate CO_2 eq. emissions, 2012

Total CO_2 emissions from energy combustion (million tons)	**264.83**
AG: Agriculture	3.48
CO: Coal	2.58
PG: Oil and gas	
MI: Other mining	
PE: Refined petroleum	4.66
CH: Chemicals	5.40
CE: Cement	27.06
IS: Iron and steel	7.98
PA: Paper and print	1.22
FD: Food processing	2.98
TE: Textiles, clothing	0.02
MW: Machinery, white Goods	0.06
ET: Electronics	2.34
AU: Automotive	0.00
EL: Electricity	119.36
CN: Construction	1.83
TR: Transportation	64.55
OE: Other economy	21.30
Total CO_2 emissions by households	**56.48**
Total CO_2 emissions from industrial processes	**41.81**
Cement	30.28
Iron and Steel	9.90
Chemicals	1.63
Total GHG emissions (CO_2 eq.)	**84.33**
CH_4 from industrial production	58.03
NO_2 from agricultural processes	21.12
F gasses from waste	5.18
Total CO_2 eq.	**447.45**

ment, which is informal (unregistered employment that is under any social security coverage) + self-employed + unpaid family labor. Using this criteria, a total of 24,819 thousand workers was distributed across regions and sectors (using the HLFS TurkStat data). Table 4.5 shows parametrization of the labor markets.

The I/O wage and salary data is used to set the formal labor share in national income. Using this data, we used the formal and informal employment shares from the HLFS data to produce aggregate wage income data for the informal labor. Finally, the sectorial and regional wage remunerations across labor types were obtained using the sectorial income shares from the I/O table. All data is summarized in Table 4.5.

Table 4.5 Parameters of the labor market, 2012

				Labor employment (thousand workers)				Total wages (Million TRY, 2012)			
				High-income region		Low-income region		High-income region		Low-income region	
		Nace 2.0	Total labor	Formal labor	Informal labor	Formal labor	Informal labor	Formal labor	Informal labor	Formal labor	Informal labor
1	AG: Agriculture	A–01, 02, 03	6,097.000	692.000	2,493.000	307.211	2,606.789	1,195.328	1,090.099	208.377	700.545
2	CO: Coal	B–05	51.024	34.925	4.939	9.778	1.383	2,328.745	93.190	493.105	16.037
3	PG+OM: Petroleum gas and other mining	B–06 + 07 + 08	79.884	54.679	7.732	15.308	2.165	1,843.365	99.038	395.472	12.862
5	PE: Refined petroleum	C–19	10.042	6.874	0.972	1.924	0.272	366.157	23.386	97.604	3.037
6	CH: Chemicals	C–20 + 21 + 22	365.705	216.649	69.065	47.157	32.834	7,085.441	876.576	1,261.741	193.306
7	CE: Cement	C–23	294.571	174.508	55.631	37.984	26.448	4,525.285	559.846	805.841	123.460
8	IS: Iron and steel	C–24	154.330	91.428	29.146	19.900	13.856	3,660.782	452.894	651.894	99.874
9	PA: Paper and print	C–17 + 18	148.416	87.924	28.029	19.138	13.325	2,180.570	269.769	388.305	59.491
10	FD: Food processing	C–10 + 11 + 12	594.080	351.942	112.195	76.605	53.338	10,089.067	1,248.170	1,796.612	275.252
11	TE: Textiles and clothing	C–13 + 14 + 15	1,267.238	750.731	239.324	163.407	113.777	14,792.422	1,830.046	2,634.163	403.569
12	MW: Machinery and white goods	C–25 + 28	647.672	383.690	122.316	83.516	58.150	8,891.314	1,099.990	1,583.322	242.574

(Continued)

Table 4.5 Parameters of the labor market, 2012 (Cont.)

| | Nace 2.0 | Labor employment (thousand workers) | | | | | Total wages (Million TRY, 2012) | | | |
| | | Total labor | High-income region | | Low-income region | | High-income region | | Low-income region | |
			Formal labor	Informal labor	Formal labor	Informal labor	Formal labor	Informal labor	Formal labor	Informal labor
13	ET: Electronics C–26 + 27	208.502	123.520	39.376	26.886	18.720	4,207.022	520.472	749.166	114.777
14	AU: Automotive C–29	208.398	123.458	39.357	26.872	18.711	3,880.834	480.118	691.080	105.878
15	EL: Electricity D–35	218.000	129.146	41.170	28.111	19.573	2,933.647	81.741	434.085	36.580
16	CN: Construction F	1,709.000	688.059	570.927	245.941	204.073	16,030.766	6,370.533	3,893.117	2,143.484
17	TR: Transportation H–49 + 50 + 51 + 53	941.559	485.223	208.405	173.439	74.493	15,778.075	695.419	1,334.800	187.606
18	OE: Other economy 09 + 16 + 30 + 31 + 32 + 33 + 36 + 37 + 38 + 39 + 4 + 5 + 46 + 47 + 52 + I + J + M + N + P + Q + R + S	11,823.579	6,660.124	2,050.071	2,234.649	878.735	265,910.609	9,107.471	22,896.581	2,946.338
	Total	24,819.000	11,054.878	6,111.655	3,517.826	4,136.641	365,699.429	24,898.757	40,315.266	7,664.670

Source: Authors' calculations from TurkStat, Household Labor Force Surveys.

REFERENCES

Acar, S.,Yeldan,A.E., March 2016. Environmental impacts of coal subsidies in Turkey: a general equilibrium analysis. Energy Policy 90, 1–15.

Agénor, P.R., 2004. Macroeconomic adjustment and the poor: analytical issues and cross-country evidence. J. Econ. Surv. 18 (3), 351–408.

Agénor, P.-R., Izquierdo, A., Fofack, H., 2003. IMMPA: A Quantitative Macroeconomic Framework for the Analysis of Poverty Reduction Strategies. World Bank Policy Research Working Paper 3092. World Bank, Washington, DC.

Akın-Ölçüm, G.,Yeldan, E., 2013. Economic impact assessment of Turkey's post-Kyoto vision on emission trading. Energy Policy 60, 764–774.

Alzua, M.L., Ruffo, H., 2011. Effects of Argentina's Social Security Reform on Labor Markets and Poverty. MPIA Working Paper 2011-11.

Armington, P., 1969. A theory of demand for products distinguished by place of production. IMF Staff Pap. 16 (1), 159–178.

Bergman, L., 1990. The development of computable general equilibrium modeling. In: Bergman, L.J., Jorgenson, D.W., Zalai, E. (Eds.), General Equilibrium Modelling and Economic Policy Analysis. Basil Blackwell Press, pp. 3–30.

Bhattacharyya, S.C., 1996. Applied general equilibrium models for energy studies: a survey. Energy Econ. 18, 145–164.

Boeters, S., Savard, L., 2012. The labor market in computable general equilibrium models. Dixon, P., Jorgenson, D. (Eds.), Handbook of CGE Modeling, vol. 1b, North Holland.

Böhringer, C., 1998. The synthesis of bottom-up and top-down in energy modeling. Energy Econ. 20, 234–248.

Böhringer, C., Löschel, A., 2006. Computable general equilibrium models of sustainability impact assessment: status qua and prospects. Ecol. Econ. 60, 49–64.

de Melo, J.A.P., 1977. Distortions in the factor market: some general equilibrium estimates. Rev. Econ. Stat. 59 (4), 398–405.

Donaghy, K.P., 2009. CGE modeling in space: a survey. In: Capello, R., Nijkamp, P. (Eds.), Handbook of Regional Growth and Development Theories. Edward Elgar, Cheltenham.

Giesecke, J.A., Madden, J.R., 2012. Regional computable general equilibrium modeling. Dixon, P., Jorgenson, D. (Eds.), Handbook of CGE Modeling, vol. 1a, North Holland.

Gilbert, J., Wahl, T., 2002. Applied general equilibrium assessments of trade liberalization in China. World Econ. 25, 697–731.

Graafland, J.J., de Mooij, R.A., Nibbelink, A.G.H., Nieuwenhuis, A., 2001. MIMICing Tax Policies and the Labor Market. Elsevier, Amsterdam.

Harris, J.R., Todaro, M.P., 1970. Migration, unemployment and development: a two-sector analysis. Am. Econ. Rev. 60 (1), 126–142.

Hendy, R., Zaki, C., 2013. Assessing the effects of trade liberalization on wage inequalities in Egypt: a microsimulation analysis. Int. Trade J. 27 (1), 63–104.

Higgins, B., 1956. The 'Dualistic Theory' of Underdeveloped Areas. Economic Development and Cultural Change 4 (2), 99–115.

Jorgenson, D.W., 1961. The development of a dual economy. Econ. J. 71 (282), 309–334.

Jorgenson, D.W., 1966. Testing alternative theories of the development of a dual economy. In: Adelman, I., Thorbecke, E. (Eds.), The Theory and Design of Economic Development. Johns Hopkins, Baltimore.

Jorgenson, D.W., 1967. Surplus Agricultural Labor and the Development of a Dual Economy. Oxford Economic Papers, Oxford, pp. 288–312.

Khan, H.A., 2004. Using Macroeconomic Computable General Equilibrium Models for Assessing Poverty Impact of Structural Adjustment Policies, Asian Development Bank Institute Discussion Paper No. 12.

Kraybill, D.S., 1993. Computable general equilibrium analysis at the regional level. In: Otto, D.M., Johnson, T.G. (Eds.), Microcomputer-based Input-Output Modeling: Applications to Economic Development. Westview Press, Boulder.

Kumbaroğlu, G.S., 2003. Environmental taxation and economic effects: a computable general equilibrium analysis for Turkey. J. Policy Model. 25, 795–810.

Lewis, W.A., 1954. Economic Development with Unlimited Supplies of Labour. Manchester School 22 (2), 139–191.

Lise, W., 2006. Decomposition of CO_2 emissions over 1980–2003 in Turkey. Energy Policy 34, 1841–1852.

Manne, A.S., 1981. ETA-MACRO: A User's Guide. Electric Power Research Institute, Palo Alto, CA.

Morrone, H., 2016. Brazilian's structural change and economic performance: structuralist comments on macroeconomic policies. Econ. Aplic. 20 (4), 473–488.

Partridge, M.D., Rickman, D.S., 2010. Computable general equilibrium (CGE) modeling for regional economic development analysis. Reg. Stud. 44, 1311–1328.

Pyatt, G., Round, J., 1979. Accounting and fixed price multipliers in a social accounting matrix framework. Econ. J. 89, 850–873.

Rada, C., von Armin, R., 2014. India's structural transformation and role in the world economy. J. Policy Model. 36 (1), 1–23.

Ranis, G., Fei, J.D.H., 1961. A theory of economic development. Am. Econ. Rev. 51, 533–565.

Roson, R., van der Mensbrugghe, J., 2017. Demand-Driven Structural Change in Applied General Equilibrium Models. IEFE Working Papers 96, IEFE, Center for Research on Energy and Environmental Economics and Policy, Universita' Bocconi, Milano, Italy.

Şahin, Ş., 2004. An Economic Policy Discussion of the GHG Emission Problem in Turkey From a Sustainable Development Perspective Within a Regional General equilibrium Model: TURCO (unpublished Ph.D. thesis). Université Paris I Panthéon, Sorbonne, submitted.

Shoven, J.B., Whalley, J., 1992. Applying General Equilibrium. Cambridge University Press, London.

Stifel, D.C., Thorbecke, E., 2003. A dual-dual CGE model of an archetype African economy: trade reform, migration and poverty. J. Policy Model. 25 (3), 207–235.

Sue Wing, I., 2004. CGE Models for Economy-Wide Policy Analysis. MIT Joint Program on the Science and Policy of Global Change, Technical Note No. 6.

Telli, Ç., Voyvoda, E., Yeldan, E., 2008. Economics of environmental policy in Turkey: a general equilibrium investigation of the economic evaluation of sectoral emission reduction policies for climate change. J. Policy Model. 30 (1), 321–340.

Temple, J.R.W., 2004. Dualism and Aggregate Productivity. CEPR Discussion Paper 4387.

Temple, J.R.W., 2005. Dual economy models: a primer for growth economists. Manch. Sch. 73 (4), 435–478.

Thorbecke, E., 1993. Impact of state and civil institutions on the operation of rural market and nonmarket configurations. World Dev. 21 (4), 591–605.

UNFCCC, 2013. GHG Inventories (Annex I), National Inventory Submissions 2013. National Report for Turkey. Available from: http://unfccc.int/national_reports/annex_i_ghg_inventories/national_inventories_submissions/itms/8108.php.

Vural, B., 2009. General Equilibrium Modeling of Turkish Environmental Policy and the Kyoto Protocol (unpublished MA thesis). Bilkent University, submitted.

Yang, Y., Huang, Y., 1997. The Impact of Trade Liberalization on Income Distribution in China. Economics Division China Economy Working Paper 97/1.

Yeldan, A.E., Taşçı, K., Voyvoda, E., Özsan, M.E., March 2013. Escape from the Middle Income Trap: Which Turkey? TURKONFED, Istanbul.

Yeldan, A.E., Taşçı, K., Özsan, M.E., Voyvoda, E., 2014. Planning for regional development: a general equilibrium analysis for Turkey. In: Yülek, M. (Ed.), Advances in General Equilibrium Modeling. Springer, pp. 291–331.

FURTHER READING

Voyvoda, E., Yeldan, E.A., 2011. Investigation of the Rational Steps Towards National Programme for Climate Change Mitigation (in Turkish). TR Ministry of Development, Ankara, mimeo.

CHAPTER 5

Policy Analysis: Toward a Green Development Pathway for the Peripheral World

The key objectives of this chapter are to address the issues of duality and informalization as characterized by peripheral development. The main aim is to identify the set of viable environmental policies against climate change within general equilibrium analytics, constrained by peripheral development. The computable general equilibrium (CGE) apparatus will be utilized as a social laboratory device to provide "what if?" characterizations across various fiscal-cum-environmental instruments of abatement control, and as a comprehensive strategy toward a more equitable and sustained development pathway.

It should be noted that the framework consistently emphasizes on regional diversification and dual relations of production and accumulation along with fragmented labor markets; rather than treating the Turkish national economy as a whole homogeneous unit, it seeks to intervene in a heterogeneous structure both location and sector wise.

The first section investigates the basic characteristics of the business-as-usual (BAU) pathway for the Turkish economy under the given policy framework and historical trends into the 2040s. An alternative green development pathway is then invoked to identify the applicable instruments for emission abatement and improved social welfare within a more equitable framework. The chapter closes with an overall discussion, concluding comments, and an epilogue to attain lessons for the developing world at large.

5.1 INCEPTION OF THE BUSINESS-AS-USUAL

In the applied general equilibrium literature, the evaluation of alternative policies is generally portrayed and studied with reference to a base-run reference (BAU) scenario. This reference scenario is important for depicting a well-defined and coherent path of the economy and for reflecting its major underlying characteristics. In other words, to have a consistent framework

Macroeconomics of Climate Change in a Dualistic Economy
http://dx.doi.org/10.1016/B978-0-12-813519-8.00005-4

of benchmarking, long-term dynamics of the economy must be anchored to a baseline reference scenario fed by trends in global forecasts. Such a design is also crucial for reflecting the global nature of climate change and the mitigation efforts at large.

The BAU scenario design described here largely relies on global data and projections compiled by the Climate Equity Reference Project. This project combines historical GDP and CO_2 emission intensity growth rates with projected growth rates from the IMFs biannual World Economic Outlook and from the IPCC Reports[1]. Thus the baseline scenario projected into 2018–40 takes into account the forecasts of the recently observed global productivity slowdown, and sets an average growth rate for the Turkish economy of 2.0%–2.5%.

Major assumptions followed in the framing of the BAU scenario include:

- The absence of any (additional) policy action to address the environmental concerns/responsibilities, or developmental concerns at a regional level.
- That Hicks–neutral productivity growth occurs at exogenous total factor productivity (TFP) growth rates, differentiated at sector and region levels in line with historical observations.
- Exogenous labor force growth rates and exogenous parameters of migration dynamics for both formal and informal labor.
- That wage rates are fixed across sectors for the formal labor category.
- Exogenously determined foreign capital inflows as ratios to the GDP.
- Exogenous domestic and foreign real interest rates.
- Endogenous real exchange rates under the constraint of the balance of payments.
- A fiscal policy in accordance with a policy rule of a targeted primary surplus. Domestic interest rates (net costs of domestic debt servicing) will reduce from their base-year values (8.0% in 2012) to an average of 5.0% by 2020 and 3.0% by 2030. The ratio of primary (noninterest) surplus is initially set at 0.04 (as a ratio to the GDP), then gradually reduced to 0.0 by 2021 and then kept at this level for the rest of the base path.

It should be noted that the purpose of the exercise is not to project into the future, but rather to make comparative assessments of alternative policy environments within the discipline of general equilibrium.

---

[1] See: https://climateequityreference.org/calculator-information/gdp-and-emissions-baselines/ for details of data compilation.

The major source of growth in this analytical structure originates from the gains in TFP. Kolsuz and Yeldan (2013) estimated that the average rate of TFP growth during 2000–10 was in the order of 1.1% per annum. The World Bank (2013) estimates that the average TFP growth in 2010–30 will be 0.8%. Given the lack of detailed estimates, the average TFP growth in this analytical structure was set equally (0.8%) for all urban–industrial sectors. Agricultural TFP was set at 0.15% for "low-income Turkey" and at 0.90% for its "high-income" counterpart. For the regional urban–industrial TFP rates, the low-income region industrial sector TFP was assumed at 0.60%, while the high-income region TFP was assumed to be 0.85%.

Further assumptions were made including that the rural labor supply would expand by 1.0% during 2013–30, with a gradual reduction to 0.7% by 2040. Conversely, the urban labor supply was projected to expand by 0.5% over the entire horizon. The final source of growth for the model economy is the accumulation of physical capital, which is endogenously achieved through investments (by sector of destination). Aggregate investment funds are generated through domestic and foreign savings; domestic saving is the saving from private disposable incomes (the neoclassical closure), while foreign saving is the resolution of exogenously given net foreign inflows.

Finally, all of the existing policy rates and ratios were maintained at their given levels on this dynamic path, hence the idea of "business-as-usual." Simulation of the 2012–40 period under these specifications yields the BAU trajectory. Relevant aspects of this trajectory are summarized in Table 5.1. With an average annual growth rate of around 2.5%, the economy is projected to reach a GDP level of approximately TRY 2,726.3 billion and 3,336.1 billion by 2030 and 2040, respectively (in fixed 2012 prices). However, the dualities still remain; for example, on this path the high-income region produced an average of 77.5% of the total added value, retaining around 83.8 and 69.4% of the formal and informal employment, respectively. The employment shares of the high-income region increased gradually over time due to the mild-operating migration dynamics from low- to high-income regions. The dynamics of growth fed by TFP growth and growth of the labor force led to declining unemployment rates in both regions. For example, the formal unemployment rate in high-income regions was 8.0% in 2017 and will decline to 7.0 and 6.0% by 2030 and 2040, respectively. Similarly, the formal unemployment rate in low-income region will decline to 8.9% by

Table 5.1 Macroeconomic results

	Base path					Scenario: green development pathway				
	2018	2020	2025	2030	2040	2018	2020	2025	2030	2040
High-income region total supply (billion TRYs, 2012 fixed prices)	3,065.8	3,239.3	3,651.9	4,124.0	5,184.4	3,042.2	3,137.9	3,655.3	4,089.7	5,229.9
Low-income region total supply (billion TRYs, 2012 fixed prices)	1,010.5	1,064.8	1,212.6	1,325.7	1,564.6	985.6	1,038.1	1,265.1	1,416.8	1,795.4
Total GDP (billion TRYs, 2012 fixed prices)	2,068.3	2,177.5	2,445.5	2,726.3	3,336.1	2,048.6	2,155.4	2,520.2	2,827.5	3,578.6
Real rate of GDP growth (%)	2.84	2.55	2.28	2.10	1.99	3.04	3.14	3.18	2.33	2.58
High-income region value added (billion TRYs, 2012 fixed prices)	1,321.2	1,389.0	1,553.8	1,732.2	2,127.1	1,309.5	1,358.7	1,581.0	1,752.7	2,209.1
Low-income region value added (billion TRYs, 2012 fixed prices)	386.2	406.3	457.3	505.6	610.8	381.8	397.1	469.2	519.6	653.9
Formal labor employment in high-income regions (persons)	12,755,118.7	13,153,617.1	14,048,537.2	15,105,756.5	16,819,084.3	12,663,874.1	12,922,673.9	14,374,770.4	15,404,763.0	17,646,593.2
Formal labor employment in low-income regions (persons)	3,059,398.6	3,063,525.1	3,005,269.6	2,945,405.0	2,858,412.9	3,024,080.0	3,003,627.6	3,105,970.1	3,054,293.8	3,095,952.1
Total formal labor employment, (persons)	15,814,517.3	16,217,142.2	17,053,806.8	18,051,161.5	19,677,497.1	15,687,954.1	15,926,301.5	17,480,740.5	18,459,056.8	20,742,545.2
Informal labor employment in high-income regions (persons)	7,262,586.6	7,523,562.7	8,098,588.9	8,606,561.0	9,547,700.3	7,262,655.9	7,524,027.4	8,092,088.5	8,583,874.2	9,480,447.7

Informal labor employment in low-income regions (persons)	3,671,905.8	3,645,423.3	3,646,203.1	3,712,623.9	3,926,298.1	3,671,842.0	3,644,964.3	3,652,808.4	3,736,411.9	4,000,789.8
Total informal labor employment, (persons)	10,934,492.4	11,168,985.9	11,744,792.0	12,319,184.9	13,473,998.4	10,934,497.9	11,168,991.6	11,744,896.9	12,320,286.1	13,481,237.5
Total labor employment (persons)	26,749,009.7	27,386,128.1	28,798,598.8	30,370,346.4	33,151,495.5	26,622,452.0	27,095,293.1	29,225,637.4	30,779,343.0	34,223,782.7
Informal labor migration (1,000s)	107,161.4	90,331.0	66,345.5	55,657.2	43,972.7	107,141.0	90,865.3	63,950.2	52,319.6	39,026.3
Unemployment rate, high income (%)	8.0	8.0	8.0	7.0	6.0	8.4	8.9	6.6	5.9	3.3
Unemployment rate low income (%)	13.4	11.9	9.9	8.9	8.9	14.0	12.9	8.8	7.3	4.7
Average unemployment rate (%)	9.4	9.0	8.4	7.4	6.6	9.8	9.9	7.1	6.2	3.6
Private disposable income (billion TRYs, 2012 fixed prices)	1,494.9	1,564.5	1,744.1	1,936.2	2,361.5	1,480.9	1,531.5	1,781.3	1,970.5	2,478.0
Government revenues/GDP (%)	27.9	27.9	27.9	27.9	28.0	28.0	29.1	29.1	29.4	29.5
PSBR/GDP (%)	−1.7	−2.0	−0.1	−0.1	−0.1	−1.7	−1.9	−0.1	−0.1	−0.1
Aggregate investment (billion TRYs, 2012 fixed prices)	569.5	598.7	662.6	727.2	871.0	566.6	603.2	693.3	762.6	939.8
Aggregate consumption (billion TRYs, 2012 fixed prices)	1,269.2	1,329.1	1,484.6	1,650.0	2,009.7	1,254.4	1,293.7	1,504.8	1,679.6	2,119.2
Private foreign debt/GDP (%)	45.2	50.9	63.2	72.7	85.3	45.5	51.2	60.9	70.2	80.1
Government foreign debt/GDP (%)	9.7	9.3	8.3	7.4	6.0	9.8	9.3	8.0	7.2	5.7
Current account deficit/GDP (%)	4.2	4.0	3.9	3.8	3.1	4.2	4.0	3.4	3.1	2.4

2030 and might stay around this level throughout, having reduced from 13.9% in 2017. However, the wedge between formal-to-informal wage-rate ratios persisted in both regions; in high-income regions the ratio remained around 8.3-fold, whereas in the low-income regions it might slightly increase to 6.8-fold by 2040 from 6.3-fold in 2017. The difference in informal wage rates decreased slightly throughout the period due to migration dynamics that sustain continued informal labor into the high-income region.

The rate of consumption growth and investment expenditure followed roughly similar trends, with the ratio of consumption-to-GDP maintained at 63%–65%, and investment at 24%. The public sector borrowing requirement (PSBR) ran at a surplus of approximately −2% to the GDP until 2020, before it reduced to −0.1%. The hypothesis here highlights the fiscal discipline and austerity characterizations of public macroeconomic policies. It should be noted that in the current global conjuncture, this is not simply a "local or domestic" decision, but the main fiscal policy stance is typically dictated by the conditions of the international finance corporations and rating agencies in an open economy and free capital mobility world. Under these conditions, the foreign deficit (current account deficit) gradually declines from 4.5% to the GDP in 2012 to 3.8 and 3.1% by 2030 and 2040, respectively. The gap between exports and imports is expected to narrow significantly by 2040 as a consequence. This result significantly depends on the assumption of exogenously maintaining the external terms of trade, and endogenously adjusting the real exchange given the hypothesized exogenous flows of foreign capital.

Regarding environmental indicators, total greenhouse gas (GHG) emissions are envisaged to rise from 602.4 million tons of CO_2 eq. in 2017 to 789.4 and 936.5 million tons by 2030 and 2040, respectively (Table 5.2). Similarly, annual CO_2 emissions are predicted to increase to 644.0 and 760.9 million tons by 2030 and 2040, respectively.

An aggregate CO_2 eq. emission volume of 641.7 million tons by 2040 is calculated to be the end result of combusting fuels for energy generation, while 126.4 million tons occurs due to industrial processes. Emissions from agricultural processes and household consumption were 118.6 and 130.3 million tons, respectively. Carbon efficiency remained around 0.40 kg/$GDP. Overall, carbonization of the Turkish economy is observed to closely follow the projected path of the real GDP. Therefore the warranted decoupling of carbonization from GDP activity is unlikely to be realized over the 2018–40 BAU path (Fig. 5.1).

Table 5.2 Environmental results

	Base path					Scenario: green development pathway[a]				
	2018	2020	2025	2030	2040	2018	2020	2025	2030	2040
Total CO_2 (million tons)	490.0	521.4	590.7	644.0	760.9	460.6	414.4	493.0	509.7	614.7
Total CO_2 eq. (million tons)	602.4	638.9	722.4	789.4	936.5	573.0	531.3	630.2	665.6	814.1
High income, CO_2 emissions from coal burning for energy (million tons)	32.9	35.2	40.1	43.5	50.6	16.5	12.5	15.5	16.5	20.9
Low income, CO_2 emissions from coal burning for energy (million tons)	8.1	8.8	10.4	11.9	15.2	4.1	3.1	3.9	4.3	6.0
High income, CO_2 energy related (million tons)	267.4	283.8	316.7	336.9	378.5	250.4	219.4	255.9	254.8	290.1
Low income, CO_2 energy related (million tons)	79.0	85.3	100.3	110.5	132.9	73.9	67.6	84.1	88.0	108.6
High income, CO_2 industrial processes (million tons)	52.5	56.1	64.3	73.4	94.4	52.3	53.5	63.6	70.0	90.6
Low income, CO_2 industrial processes (million tons)	15.9	16.8	19.2	21.0	24.8	15.3	15.9	19.7	21.6	27.6
High income, CO_2 eq. agriculture (million tons)	37.0	38.3	42.6	47.9	60.4	36.6	37.7	42.5	48.2	61.3
Low income, CO_2 eq. agriculture (million tons)	40.4	42.3	47.6	51.2	58.2	41.2	43.7	53.2	61.2	79.0
CO_2 households (million tons)	75.2	79.4	90.3	102.2	130.3	68.7	58.0	69.8	75.3	97.7
Total CO_2 energy related (million tons)	421.6	448.5	507.3	549.5	641.7	392.9	345.0	409.7	418.1	496.5
Total CO_2/GDP (kg/$GDP)	0.4	0.4	0.4	0.4	0.4	0.4	0.3	0.4	0.3	0.3
CO_2 from energy/GDP (kg/$GDP)	0.4	0.4	0.4	0.4	0.3	0.3	0.3	0.3	0.3	0.2

(Continued)

Table 5.2 Environmental results (*cont.*)

	Base path					Scenario: green development pathway[a]				
	2018	2020	2025	2030	2040	2018	2020	2025	2030	2040
Intermediate demand coal in low income (billion TRYs, 2012 fixed prices)	2.8	3.0	3.4	4.0	5.4	1.3	0.9	1.2	1.3	2.0
Intermediate demand coal in high income (billion TRYs, 2012 fixed prices)	11.6	12.5	14.9	17.4	23.7	5.2	3.8	5.0	5.7	8.4
Intermediate demand petrol and gas in low income (billion TRYs, 2012 fixed prices)	24.4	26.1	30.4	35.0	45.8	24.0	18.1	22.8	23.1	31.8
Intermediate demand petrol and gas in high income (billion TRYs, 2012 fixed prices)	95.5	103.5	124.1	147.0	207.9	96.2	73.8	93.1	95.0	130.4
Intermediate demand ref. petrol in low income (billion TRYs, 2012 fixed prices)	21.5	22.7	26.2	28.9	34.5	20.9	21.6	26.6	29.7	38.0
Intermediate demand ref. petrol in high income (billion TRYs, 2012 fixed prices)	60.14	63.41	71.22	80.28	100.95	59.58	60.37	69.95	77.82	99.22

[a] Green development pathway = remove coal subsidies + impose CO_2 taxes + earmark CO_2 tax revenues to expanded investments on renewables + increase the efficiency of aggregate energy composites.

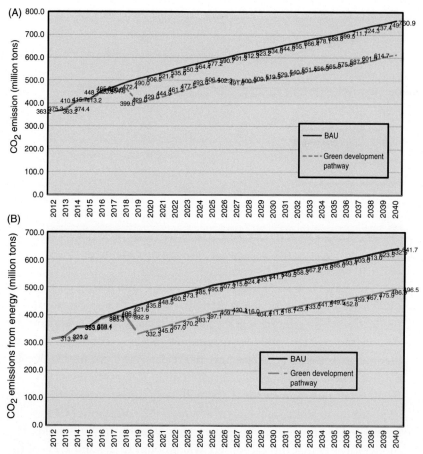

Figure 5.1 *(A) CO$_2$ emission trajectories BAU and green development pathway (million tons). (B) CO$_2$ emission from energy (million tons).*

5.2 INSTRUMENTS OF THE GREEN DEVELOPMENT PATHWAY

Next, the analytical model described in Chapter 4 was used to investigate the macroeconomic impacts of a policy package that aims to set a green development policy for a typical middle-income country. This policy package is fenced-in under the constraints of climate change mitigation and under the need to achieve balanced and sustained development.

The implementation of the policy package is comprised of four main instruments:

1. **Elimination of coal subsidies:** The first instrument comprises the elimination of coal production subsidies (which amount to approximately 0.1%

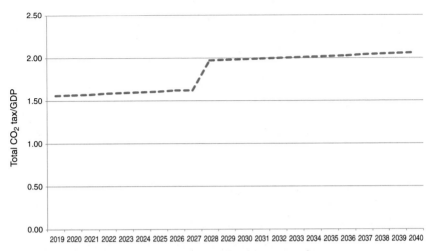

Figure 5.2 *Total CO$_2$ taxes/GDP under green development pathway.*

of GDP), as well as some regional investment subsidies on coal mining (which are supported by the central government to boost regional coal production). The existing scheme subsidizes the cost of investments by 30 and 35% in high- and low-income regions, respectively, via reduced income or corporate taxes (see Acar and Yeldan (2016) for further details).

2. Carbon taxation: This policy instrument is a dynamically-active and flexible taxation scheme on CO$_2$ polluters. In the model, this tax is imposed on an ad valorem basis as a ratio of the emissions of CO$_2$ as differentiated by the source of polluters, energy users, and households. The model foresees that this carbon tax will amount to 2.0 and 2.1% of the GDP by 2030 and 2040, respectively (Fig. 5.2).

3. Renewable energy investment fund: The third policy instrument is a fiscal policy intervention to earmark the total tax proceeds from carbon taxation to an investment fund for the expansion of renewables. Here, an asymmetrical treatment of the regions is assumed in order to associate this new investment prospect with the developmental needs of the low-income region. Thus 60% of the total funding is afforded to this relatively backward region.

4. Energy efficiency: The final policy instrument entails autonomous increase in energy efficiency (i.e., depending on technological advances and market conditions and not on any deliberate supporting efficiency policy). It is assumed that this policy instrument will gradually facilitate a higher per unit energy output (an annual increase from 0.5% to 1.5%) from primary and secondary energy sources.

5.2.1 Removal of Fossil Fuel Subsidies

Coal is still a widely used energy source in the international arena. Data from the International Energy Agency (IEA, 2014) revealed that the share of coal in world electricity production rose from 37.4% to 40.3% between 1990 and 2012. Some of this production was due to the availability of generous subsidies provided by governments to their coal sectors. These subsidies are usually designed to lower the cost of coal-fired electricity production, increase the price received by energy producers, or decrease the price paid by energy consumers. They take several forms including direct financial transfers, tax exemptions, market-price support, and the provision of services below market rates (i.e., the provision of land, water, infrastructure, or permissions) based on the WTO definition. The cost of global fossil fuel subsidies (FFS) (i.e., oil, gas, and coal subsidies) totaled USD 548 billion in 2013, which was 4 times more than renewable energy subsidies (IEA, 2014).

In 2009 the G20 leaders committed to "rationalize and phase out over the medium term inefficient FFS that encourage wasteful consumption." This engagement has since been endorsed by the Asia-Pacific Economic Cooperation (APEC, 2009; Leaders' Declaration). The topic of FFS is currently gaining momentum in a post-Rio+20 context, and the reform of "environmentally harmful subsidies" is also part of the Europe 2020 strategy. Withana et al. (2012) categorized such subsidies in the EU member states as on- and off-budget subsidies. Examples include direct financing for hard coal mining being phased out under state aid rules (e.g., in Denmark, Spain, Poland, and the United Kingdom); energy tax reductions for the manufacturing, agricultural, and forestry sectors; and tax exemptions for certain energy-intensive processes (e.g., in Denmark).

Studies that have investigated the possible socioeconomic and environmental impacts of FFS have mostly focused on scenarios to understand the impact of reduction, full elimination, or reformulation of subsidies. Ellis (2010) reviewed subsidy reduction scenarios in six different studies and found that reform would lead to a significant global increase in income and a decrease in CO_2 emissions[2]. For instance, considering OECD and non-OECD countries in a multiregional dynamic general equilibrium study, Burniaux et al. (1992) estimated that full global FFS removal would lead to an 18% reduction in CO_2 emissions in 2050 compared to the base path. They also stated that annual real income increases from the removal of all

---

[2] For detailed findings of the six studies referred to by Ellis (2010) see: https://www.iisd.org/gsi/sites/default/files/effects_ffs.pdf.

consumer FFS would be 0.7% globally, 0.1% for OECD countries, and 1.6% for non-OECD countries over the 1990–2050 period (Ellis, 2010, p. 40).

Utilizing a CGE framework for the analysis of FFS in Vietnam, a UNDP (2012) study showed that the elimination of subsidies would increase actual GDP by 1% and significantly decrease GHG emissions. Moreover, a subsidy cut alongside a carbon tax scenario would bring about a 1.5% increase in GDP and considerably higher investment rates compared to the BAU scenario over the period to 2020. The CGE model used in the study assumed that revenue savings and increases were invested in the most productive sectors or in low-carbon activities (i.e., R&D).

Existing coal subsidies decrease the competitiveness of renewable energy technologies, jeopardize renewable energy investments, and ensure that energy systems are dependent on fossil fuel-based energy generation (i.e., "lock-in") (Bridle and Kitson, 2014). A climate policy that aims to limit the global temperature increase to 2°C requires governments to completely abandon fossil fuels (i.e., coal, petrol, and natural gas). If the subsidies provided to such sectors are eliminated, most "polluting" projects would likely be abandoned and investments would shift to other sectors. Analyses conducted by CTI (2013) suggested that this sectoral transformation and renunciation of subsidies would lead to a gross loss of earnings of USD 28 trillion for the fossil fuel industry by 2035, and large volumes of fossil fuels would remain idle as stranded assets. Therefore even though they have not reached the end of their economic life span, existing coal and fossil fuels wouldbecome idle, as they would be unable to bring in income in a world that had transitioned to a low-carbon economy. The latest calculations indicate that 80% of the coal, petrol, and natural gas reserves held by large-scale companies have already been marked as "unburnable carbon" due to the threat of climate change (CTI, 2013).

FFS in Turkey mainly comprise of coal subsidies. Acar et al. (2015) recorded that the most substantial coal subsidies are direct transfers from the Undersecretariat of the treasury to the hard coal sector, usually in the form of capital and duty-loss payments. These transfers aim to subsidize local employment in the hard coal-mining regions and amounted to around USD 300 million in 2013. The government also supports the coal sector by providing R&D expenditure, funding the rehabilitation of hard coal mines and coal power stations, providing exploration budgets, funding new coal power plants, providing investment guarantees to some coal power plants, and distributing free coal to poor families as consumer support. The total quantifiable coal subsidies in Turkey in 2013 amounted to USD 730 million; however, some of the support measures remain unquantifiable as they are not purely financial transfer mechanisms. For instance, exemptions from environmental regulations (including temporary exemptions for existing coal plants) and permissive environmental impact assessments enable most coal projects to be implemented even though they are harmful to the environment (Acar et al., 2015, pp. 8–11). In addition, Turkey introduced a new investment incentive scheme in 2012, which was composed of various instruments including VAT and customs duty exemption, income or corporate tax reduction, social security premium support to the employer, interest support, and land allocation. Defined as "priority areas," new coal mining and power generation projects were subsidized within the regional investment incentive scheme with the most generous measures.

Using the data for quantifiable incentives in 2013, Acar et al. (2015) estimated that the producer subsidy for coal amounted to USD 0.01 per kWh, which increased to USD 0.02 per kWh when coal aid to the consumer was included. Needless to say, these figures serve as an underestimate of the total subsidy, as they do not cover incentives, such as investment guarantees, ease of credit access, exemption from value-added tax, exemption from import duties (within the regional investment incentive scheme), or any of the other identified subsidies.

Acar and Yeldan (2016) examined the macroeconomic and environmental impacts of coal subsidies in Turkey within a general equilibrium framework. They established that if the production and investment subsidies provided to coal are eliminated by 2030, CO_2 emissions will decrease significantly in both high- and low-income regions. In such a scenario, a national emission reduction of 5.4% would be realized in 2030 when compared to the base path. Given that the coal sector comprises only a small portion of the sectoral composition of the country, it is clear that eliminating the coal subsidies would be beneficial in terms of combating environmental damage and climate change.

Estimates from other scientific reports (Fraunhofer ISE, 2013) further confirm that coal power will remain a less-expensive technology than renewable energy, although renewable technologies are expected to get cheaper in the coming decades. However, taking advantage of these falling costs is likely to prove difficult if the energy sector has already configured its technical and institutional structure to support coal-fired generation and if financial support to the coal industry has become part of the status quo. This may lead to the danger of path dependence (i.e., firms becoming "locked" in dirty technologies). Given the distorted prices, firms with a history of dirty innovations may be further led toward maintaining dirty technologies and creating path dependence in the long run (Aghion, 2014).

Thus the green development scenario exclusively aims to break away from the fossil fuel-based energy-production technologies, and it attempts to accommodate the warranted technological changes via making savings from the elimination of FFS and the (yet to be implemented) carbon tax monies.

5.2.2 Taxing Carbon

The second policy instrument is the taxation of carbon emissions to be imposed at the source. To make the issue explicit, the OECD definition will be utilized, which states that "carbon taxes is a form of explicit carbon pricing; referring to a tax directly linked to the level of carbon emissions, often expressed as a value per tonne CO_2 equivalent" (OECD, 2013). Carbon taxes have the advantage of being explicit and having defined coverage; however, one disadvantage is that the level of abatement (the expected rate of emission reduction) is not predefined. Nevertheless, carbon taxation is a significant part of the arsenal of environmental policy instruments in a number of countries. For example, Denmark and Finland adopted a form of a carbon tax as early as 1990. The Danish carbon tax encompasses the combustion of fossil fuels, with a partial exemption for sectors that participate in the EU Emission Trading System; the Finnish tax system mostly operates using a combination of carbon and energy tax. As of 2014 the Danish and Finnish tax rates were USD 31 and EUR 35 per ton of CO_2 eq. respectively (World Bank, 2014). Similar policies are seen in other countries, such as France, Ireland, Mexico, Norway, Sweden, and Switzerland, where the tax rates per ton of CO_2 eq. are USD 10, EUR 20, MXN 10–50, USD 4–69, USD 168, and USD 68, respectively (all 2014 levels).

Goulder (1995) analyzed the costs of carbon taxes via a model that entails interactions between the carbon tax and preexisting taxes in the US economy. It was determined that the costs of such carbon tax policies are significantly reduced when the proceeds of the carbon tax are utilized to finance income tax cuts. It was also acknowledged that the costs of carbon tax are sensitive to the level of preexisting taxes. Therefore any environmental tax policy should consider the feedback effects with regards to preexisting taxes in other sectors of the economy.

Devarajan et al. (2011) modeled the South African economy within the CGE framework to test the effects of several tax policy scenarios that would produce a 15% decline in CO_2 emissions. They showed that a carbon tax would produce the lowest marginal cost of abatement. The authors concluded that the costs of such environmental taxation would be even lower if the labor market distortions in South Africa could be overcome.

Yahoo and Othman (2017) framed a CGE model that focused on the energy–emission relationship in Malaysia. Malaysia is a country that intends to reduce its CO_2 eq. emission intensity (% of GDP) by approximately 40% by 2020 (compared to its 2005 level). Their model aimed to assess the macroeconomic and welfare impacts of carbon and energy tax policies that are needed for the country to achieve such reductions. Their findings demonstrate that the negative economy-wide impact of carbon and energy taxes is negligible when the emission reduction is considered. Under the specified assumptions, implementation of a carbon tax appears to be the best choice, especially when the tax revenues are channeled to consumption subsidies on household purchases. The study also indicated that a carbon tax works better than an energy tax for handling emissions, as it leads to higher use of renewable energy in Malaysia.

A Turkish study by Kolsuz and Yeldan (2017) used an applied general equilibrium model to focus on the interrelationship between environmental abatement instruments and policies. It showed that Turkey can achieve a proemployment, eco-friendly, and sustained growth path by using an appropriate mix of environmental taxes and technological innovations. The authors channeled tax revenues to a wage fund, which was used to finance the so-called "green jobs" sector, therefore environmental abatement was achievable via eco-friendly employment. The effects of new carbon-mitigation technologies and endogenous technological innovations were also examined. This scenario projected a 19.7% reduction of total CO_2 eq. emissions by 2030 when compared to the base path. This analysis further proves that halving the existing labor taxes can help to successfully mitigate carbon emissions (Kolsuz and Yeldan, 2017).

These historical studies indicate that the introduction of a universal emissions tax for all polluters (enterprises as well as households) would be advantageous. As noted earlier, the tax should be imposed on an ad valorem basis as a ratio of the emissions of CO_2, as differentiated by the source of polluters, energy users, and households.

5.2.3 Investing in Renewables

In our model we distinguish 18 sectors, 17 of which are officially recognized in the official input–output (I/O) tables by TURKSTAT. The renewable energy sources (RNW) sector is not recorded in the official I/O statistics in the framework described, therefore its inclusion relies on comparative data from aggregated energy supply–use tables, data on the levelized cost of energy (LCOE) from the World Energy Association, and Bloomberg New Energy Finance (BNEF), 2014 material on energy balances (Table 5.3). From this an estimate of the market valuation of the RNW sector can be obtained.

The BNEF data suggests that 65,348.8 (GWh) of RNW were utilized in the production of electricity in Turkey in 2012 (the base year). This equates to 27.3% of the energy used for producing electricity (Table 5.3). The coal and petroleum–gas sectors used 28.4 and 44.3% of the total energy for electricity production, respectively. The LCOE estimates from the Bloomberg data were used to convert these energy balances into "market values." The ratio of RNW to coal market value was then used to obtain a value item to be utilized in the social accounting matrix, 2012. This exercise yielded a value of TRY 2,247.1 million (in fixed 2012 prices) for the renewables sector.

This exercise also provided a series of conversion ratios (e) to convert energy units into market values (i.e., RNW^{TL} [1/e] = RNW^{tJUL}). This revealed a coefficient of 0.034 (thousand TRY [2012 prices]/MWh) for the RNW sector.

Table 5.3 LCOE and top-down cost conversion coefficients in electricity production

	I/O data (2012, million TRY)	Power generation[a] (GWh)	LCOE[b] (Bloomberg data, USD/MWh)	Total value implied by TEIAS and Bloomberg LCOE (million TRY)	Conversion coefficients (Σ) implied for I/O data[c] (million TRY/GWh)
Coal	2,892.9	68,013.1	92.39	11,310.7	0.04253
Petroleum and gas (and OM)	25,263.6	106,137.9	82.00	15,666.0	0.23803
Renewables (including hydro)	2,247.08	65,345.8	74.69	8,785.7	0.03439

Input–output value of renewables is estimated via
(11310.7/8785.7) × 2,892.9 = TRY 2,247.08 million

[a] Power generation taken from TEIAS data.
[b] Levelized cost of energy (LCOE) is taken from Bloomberg data. For coal, the total production shares of lignite and hard coal are taken into account when calculating the weighted average. Likewise, the total renewables share of hydroelectricity and other RNW in power generation, along with the LCOE of each, are taken into account to calculate the weighted average.
[c] Input–output data/power generation (GWh).

The RNW sector is thought to be utilized only in the production of electricity, and is "produced" as a factor of production via investments in renewables. In the long term, as more resources are diverted to renewables production, the available investment funds will be taken away from other sectors toward the RNW sector. This is an unavoidable trade-off between CO_2 mitigation and pure growth.

5.2.4 Improving Energy Efficiency

Mitigation of climate change will not be realized through fiscal measures alone. This fact is one of the stylized facts of climate change macroeconomics, and it is appropriate to accommodate for gains in energy efficiency within the green development package. Therefore a further hypothesis was implemented to state that the efficiency policies will gradually facilitate a higher per unit energy output (an annual increase from 0.5% to 1.5%) from primary and secondary energy sources.

5.3 FINDINGS AND POLICY DISCUSSION

The macroeconomic results of the green development pathway policy package are summarized and contrasted against the BAU pathway in Table 5.1. Of prime importance is the evolution of the GDP during 2015–40. In contrast to the BAU, the green development scenario suffered a slight initial loss. The deceleration of GDP growth lasts for approximately 10 years, roughly until 2025. The GDP level in the green development scenario is 0.9% below that of BAU in 2018, and 1.01% below by 2020. The gap between the two scenarios quickly narrowed; however, the income-enhancing effects of the renewable sector allowed the green development scenario to catch up with the BAU in 2025. The green development scenario thereafter achieved rapid gains in national income due to the gains in renewables and energy efficiency that were earmarked by fiscal savings from the elimination of coal subsidization and the initiation of the carbon taxation programs. By the end of the planning horizon the green development pathway reported a real gross income of TRY 3,578.6 billion (in fixed 2012 prices), which was 7.2% greater than the BAU pathway. These gains materialize in the long term as a result of a consistent and coherent policy package simultaneously addressing both the fiscal balances and the regional equity objectives.

The gains in GDP were shared unevenly across the regions and favored the low-income regions. The value added of the low-income regions will accelerate after 2025 to achieve a regional value that was 7.1% higher under

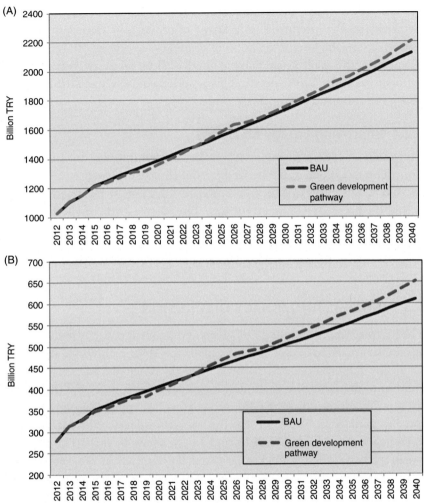

Figure 5.3 *(A) High-income region value added (bill TRY, fixed 2012 prices). (B) Low-income region value added (bill TRY, fixed 2012 prices).*

the green development policy than under the BAU scenario. Likewise, the value added in the high-income regions was 3.9% higher than under the BAU pathway (Fig. 5.3).

Of greater interest was the interregional gap. The modeling results suggest that the gap in aggregate GDP between the two regions narrowed down secularly over the green development trajectory. This achievement is partly due to the gains in formalization of the labor market in the low-income region. Formal employment in the low-income regions will rise by 8.2% by 2040, which is supported by a 4.9% increase of formal labor employment in the high-income region compared with the BAU. Elevated formal employment levels in both regions will produced a total formal employment level, that will be 5.4% higher than the BAU scenario by 2040.

The rise in employment in the high-income region resulted to a reduction in the unemployment rate to 3.3% (compared to 6.0% in BAU), and to 4.7% in the low-income region (compared with 8.9% in BAU). Therefore the average unemployment rate fell to 3.6% in 2040 in contrast to 6.6% level under the BAU scenario.

Elimination of the coal production subsidies and invigoration of the carbon taxation program led to a rise of the state's fiscal revenues and helped to improve the budget balance of the public sector. Public foreign borrowing narrows down and, together with the rise in private incomes, is coupled with a similar fall of private debt. As a result of these two favorable outcomes, the account deficit narrows down to a 2.4% ratio to GDP by 2040 (in contrast to BAUs 3.1%). Thus the green development package not only achieved a rise in incomes and employment, but also sustained a fall in foreign debt and a fall in the foreign deficit of the overall domestic economy.

The environmental indicators are summarized in Table 5.2 The evolution of the key abatement indicators are portrayed in Figs 5.3–5.6. The results reveal that aggregate emissions of total GHGs and CO_2 decreased from the beginning of the planning phase under the green development pathway. Aggregate GHGs will fall from 936.5 million tons of CO_2 eq. under BAU, to 814.1 million tons by 2040. Likewise, CO_2 emissions reduced from 760.9 to 614.7 million tons by 2040. These amount to abatement gains of 13.1 and 19%, respectively. The biggest abatement gain was seen for energy utilization. Switching from fossil fuels to renewable sources of energy generation reduced the energy-related CO_2 emissions by 22% under the green development pathway, from 641.7 to 496.5 million tons by 2040 (Fig. 5.1).

The realization of increased GDP, together with the fall in emissions, led to a fall in the emission content of national income; in other words, a decline in CO_2 per unit of \$GDP. This is a direct indicator of a more efficient structure in terms of environmental abatement. CO_2 per unit of GDP decreased from 0.4 to 0.3 kg/\$GDP, whereas energy related emissions decreased from 0.3 to 0.2 kg/USD (Fig. 5.4).

It is interesting that emissions from agricultural and industrial processes increased in the low-income regions (Table 5.2). This is due to the invigoration of productivity in the region, both in sectoral production and employment. As we do not have any intervention in abatement control

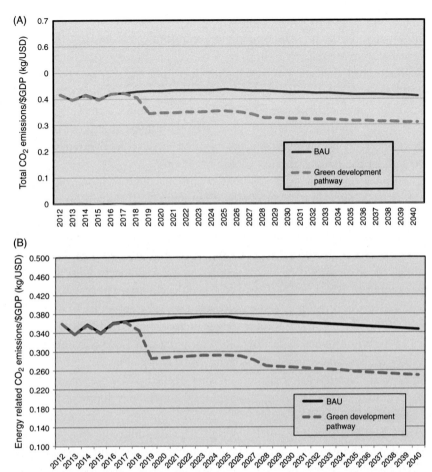

Figure 5.4 *(A) Total CO$_2$ emissions per $GDP (kg/USD) (2012 prices). (B) Energy-related CO$_2$ emissions per $GDP (kg/USD) (2012 prices).*

differentiated regionally, the rise in process activity should be regarded as normal. Nevertheless, decomposition of the aggregate CO$_2$ emissions (Fig. 5.5) showed that all sources of emissions fall under the green development pathway with respect to BAU, with the exception of industrial processes.

These gains in rationalization of abatement reveal themselves in the course of electricity generation. The green development intervention is leading to a rise of the share of renewables (solar and wind) in electricity generation from 4% in 2012 to 55% by 2040; and to a decline of coal's share from 28% to >10%. Likewise the share of petroleum and gas has been

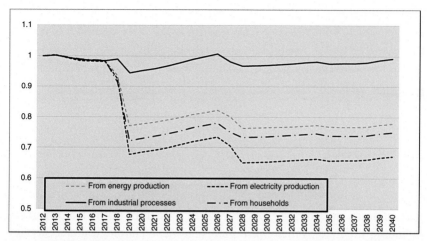

Figure 5.5 *Green development policy package: decomposition of CO_2 emissions (with respect to base path).*

declining from 44% in 2012 to 28% by 2040. In combination, the share of nonrenewable sources of electricity generation under the green development package is reducing from 72% in 2012 to 37% by 2040 (Fig. 5.6).

A critical instrument behind these gains is carbon taxation. These results indicate that with the implementation of the polluter-pays principle across producers and households, the carbon tax incidence (as a ratio to the aggregate GDP) is around 1.5% in the early periods of the green development pathway, and will secularly rise to 2.2% by 2040 (Fig. 5.2).

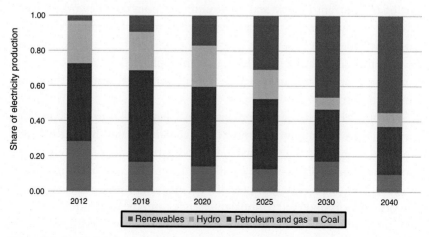

Figure 5.6 *Green development pathway: shares in electricity production.*

In contrast to the level of aggregate CO_2 emissions in 2040, this means a tax rate of 128 TRY/ton of CO_2 (in fixed 2012 prices), or 51.3 USD/ton (in real 2012 USD). Finally, in contrast to the gains in CO_2 emissions, carbon taxation results in marginal abatement costs of 540 TRY/ton of CO_2 mitigated in 2040, which is roughly 214 USD/ton of CO_2 mitigation (in constant 2012 USD).

5.4 EPILOGUE

The previous chapters have addressed the concept of development and its challenges in the 21st century, and the multilayered appearances of dualism, pertaining to and going beyond the classical dualism of the labor markets, including the heterogeneity of capital, regional technological diversity, access to knowledge capital, and integration of the world commodity and financial markets. Chapter 2 laid out how the functioning of the global economy and the trends of deindustrialization exacerbate existing challenges via stagnant wages, declining investment trends, and poor achievement of productivity growth. The issue of climate change in this picture seems to serve as yet another obstacle. On one hand, climate change creates serious development challenges; however, on the other hand, prioritizing economic growth and development have had major effects on climate change and vulnerability. Emission control and effective mitigation demand the transformation of production systems and energy systems, such as moving away from traditional high-carbon energy sources, deploying advanced renewable technologies, and increasing energy efficiency. In Chapter 3, evaluation of the current energy and environmental policy framework, and the potential implications of this framework for climate change in the Turkish economy, underlines how a lack of sufficient regional mitigation efforts and the ever increasing burden of climate responsibility relates and contributes to mounting spatial inequalities and dual economic structures within a national economy.

The model developed and presented in Chapter 4 aims to incorporate a regional general equilibrium model that accommodates the structure and dynamics of the dual traps embedded in the Turkish economy. Referred to as regional computable general equilibrium modeling, the most important contributions of this construction are the decomposition of the national economy into its observed regional differences, and the generation of a concrete impact analysis of the instruments of regional policy. Chapter 5 contained further analysis of a comprehensive package of the macroeconomic development policies that are designed at the regional level, together with those that aim to abate environmental pollution and climate change.

In conclusion, these results indicate that by pursuing a coherent macroeconomic strategy to effectively tax fossil fuel use, remove coal subsidies, and earmark fiscal revenues for the expansion of the renewables sector within regional development programs, Turkey can mitigate gaseous emissions and expand its income and employment within a more equitable and sustained development pathway. This has serious implications for developing and developed economies, as it documents that with coherent programs, abatement policies can serve as viable sources of structural change and industrialization, rather than being mutually exclusive objectives, as is often alleged.

REFERENCES

Acar, S., Kitson, L., Bridle, R., 2015. Subsidies to coal and renewable energy in Turkey. Global Subsidies Initiative Report, March 2015, IISD.

Acar, S., Yeldan, E., 2016. Environmental impacts of coal subsidies in Turkey: a general equilibrium analysis. Energy Policy 90, 1–15.

Aghion, P., 2014. Industrial policy for green growth. Paper presented at the 17th World Congress of the International Economics Association, Jordan.

Asia–Pacific Economic Cooperation (APEC), 2009. Leaders' Declaration: Sustaining growth, connecting the region. APEC Singapore Summit, Singapore, November 14–15. Available from: <http://www.apec.org/Meeting-Papers/Leaders-Declarations/2009/2009_aelm.aspx>.

Bloomberg New Energy Finance (BNEF), 2014. Turkey's changing power markets (White Paper). Bloomberg New Energy Finance. Available from: http://about.bnef.com/white-papers/turkeys-changing-power-markets/.

Bridle, R., Kitson, L., 2014. The impact of fossil-fuel subsidies on renewable electricity generation. International Institute for Sustainable Development (IISD), Global Subsidies Initiative (GSI) Report. Available from: <https://www.iisd.org/gsi/sites/default/files/ffs_rens_impacts.pdf>.

Burniaux, J.-m., Martin, J.P., Oliveira-Martins, J., 1992. The effects of existing distortions in energy markets on the costs of policies to reduce CO_2 emissions: evidence from GREEN. OECD Econ. Stud. 19, 141–165.

CTI, 2013. Unburnable Carbon 2013: wasted capital and stranded asset. London: Carbon Tracker Initiative. Available from: <http://www.carbontracker.org/wp-content/uploads/2014/09/Unburnable-Carbon-2-Web-Version.pdf>.

Devarajan, S., Go, D., Robinson, S., Thierfelder, K., 2011. Tax policy to reduce carbon emissions in a distorted economy: illustrations from a South Africa CGE model. B. E. J. Econ. Anal. Policy 11 (1).

Ellis, J., 2010. The effects of fossil-fuel subsidy reform: a review of modeling and empirical studies. International Institute for Sustainable Development (IISD), Global Subsidies Initiative (GSI). Available from: <https://www.iisd.org/gsi/sites/default/files/effects_ffs.pdf>.

Fraunhofer ISE, 2013. Levelized Cost of Electricity: Renewable Energy Technologies. Study Edition, November 2013. Available from: <http://www.ise.fraunhofer.de/en/publications/studies/cost-of-electricity>.

Goulder, L.H., 1995. Effects of carbon taxes in an economy with prior tax distortions: an intertemporal general equilibrium analysis. J. Environ. Econ. Manage. 29 (3), 271–297.

IEA, 2014. World Energy Outlook International Energy Agency. Available from: https://www.iea.org/publications/freepublications/publication/WEO2014.pdf.

Kolsuz, G.,Yeldan, E., 2013. 1980-Sonrası Türkiye Ekonomisinde Büyümenin Kaynaklarının Ayrıştırılması. Çalışma ve Toplum 40 (1), 49–66.

Kolsuz, G.,Yeldan, E., 2017. Economics of climate change and green employment: a general equilibrium investigation for Turkey. Renew. Sustain Energy Rev. 70, 1240–1250.

OECD, 2013. Taxing Energy Use—A Graphical Analysis. OECD Publishing, Paris.

UNDP, 2012. Fossil Fuel Fiscal Policies and Greenhouse Gas Emissions in Vietnam. Policy Paper. UNDP–Vietnam. Available from: <http://www.un.org.vn/en/publications/publications-by-agency/cat_view/126-un-publications-by-agency/90-undp-publications.html>.

Withana, S., ten Brink, P., Franckx, L., Hirschnitz-Garbers, M., Mayeres, I., Oosterhuis, F., Porsch, L., 2012. Study supporting the phasing out of environmentally harmful subsidies. Report by the Institute for European Environmental Policy (IEEP), Institute for Environmental Studies—Vrije Universiteit (IVM), Ecologic Institute and VITO for the European Commission—DG Environment. Final Report, Brussels.

World Bank, 2013. Turkey Green Growth Policy Paper: Towards a Greener Economy. April, Washington, DC, United States.

World Bank, 2014. Putting a price on carbon with a tax. Available from: <http://www.worldbank.org/content/dam/Worldbank/document/SDN/background-note_carbon-tax.pdf>.

Yahoo, M., Othman, J., 2017. Carbon and energy taxation for CO_2 mitigation: a CGE model of the Malaysia. Environ. Dev. Sustain. 19:239. Available from: <https://doi.org/10.1007/s10668-015-9725-z>.

INDEX

Printed in the United States
By Bookmasters